THE PICTURE BOOK OF

RAINBOWS

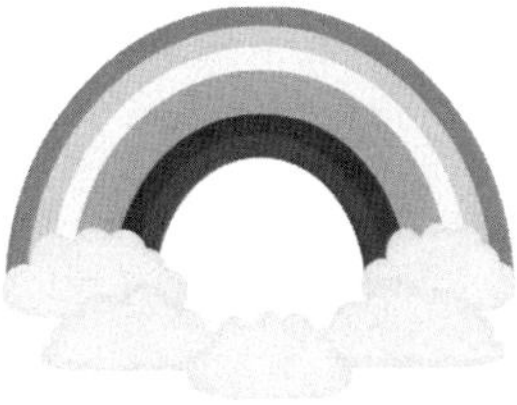

SUNNY STREET
BOOKS

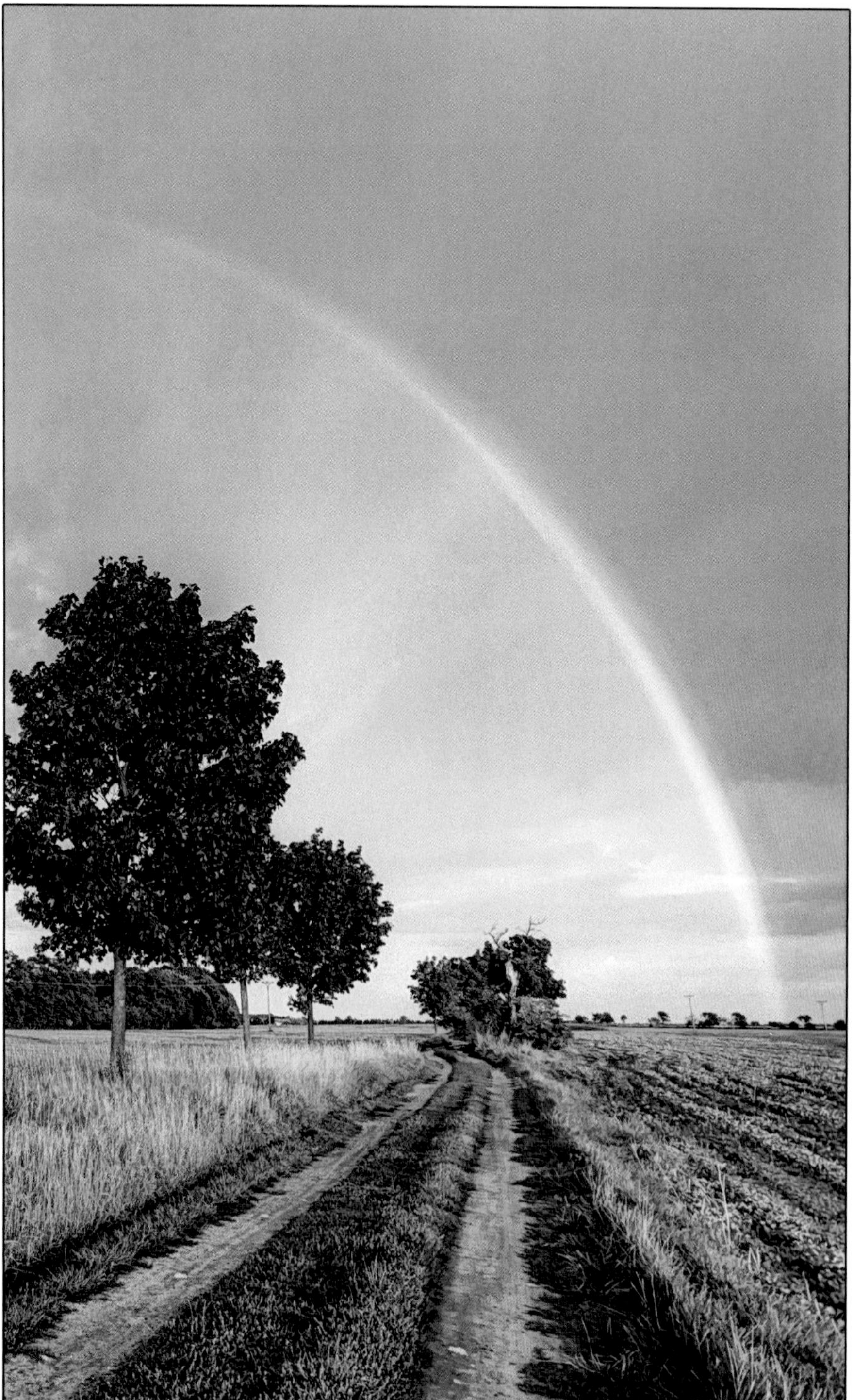

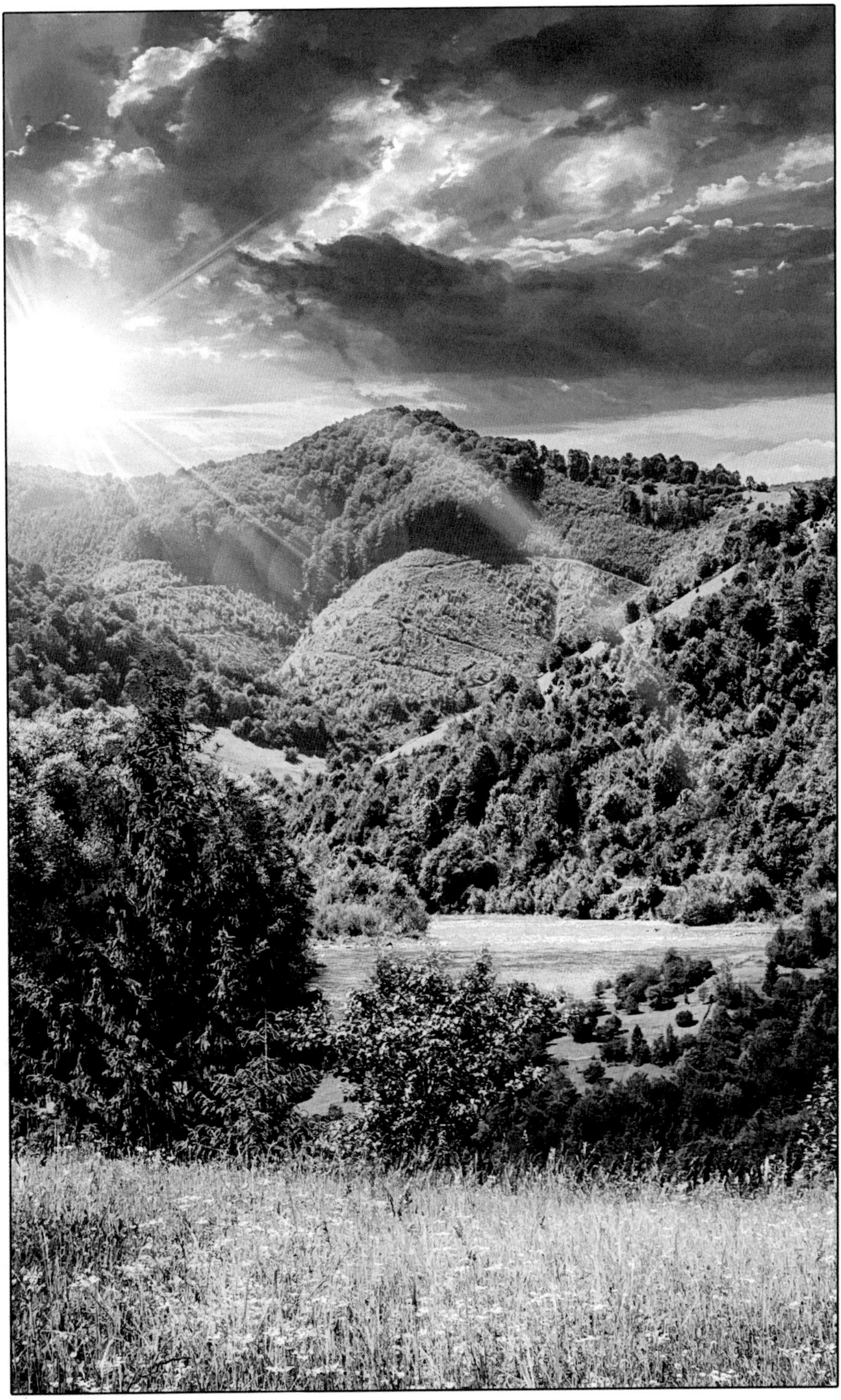

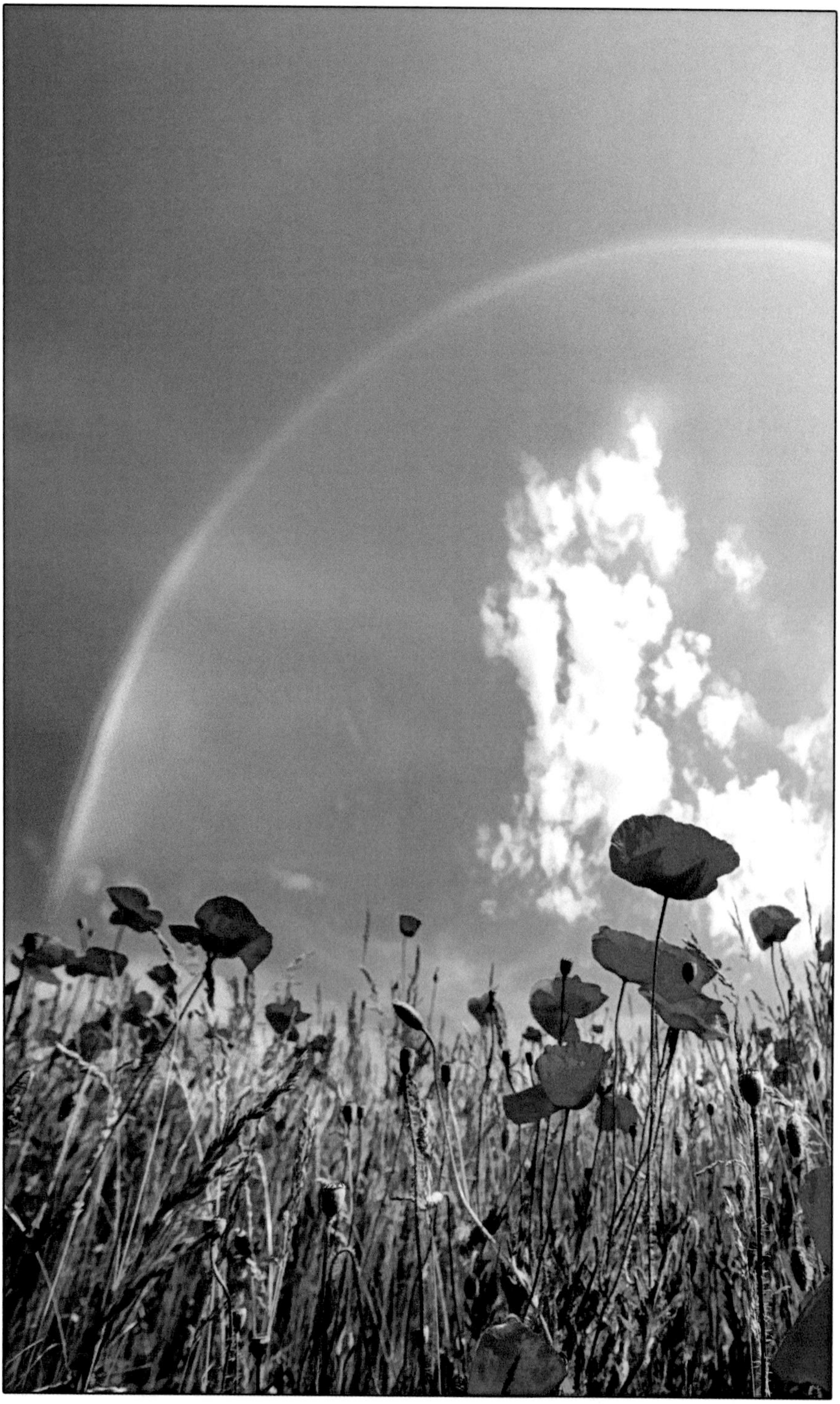

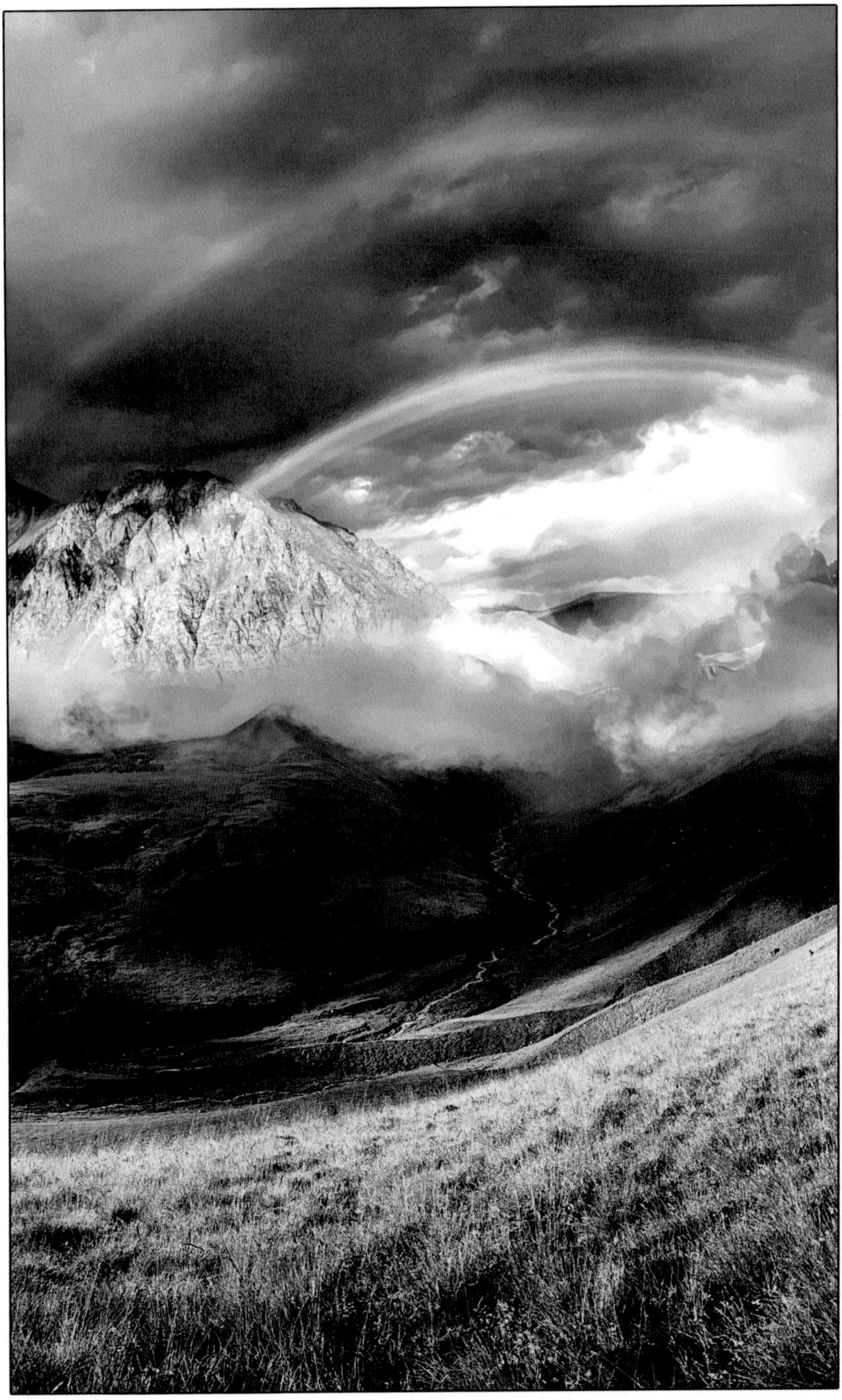

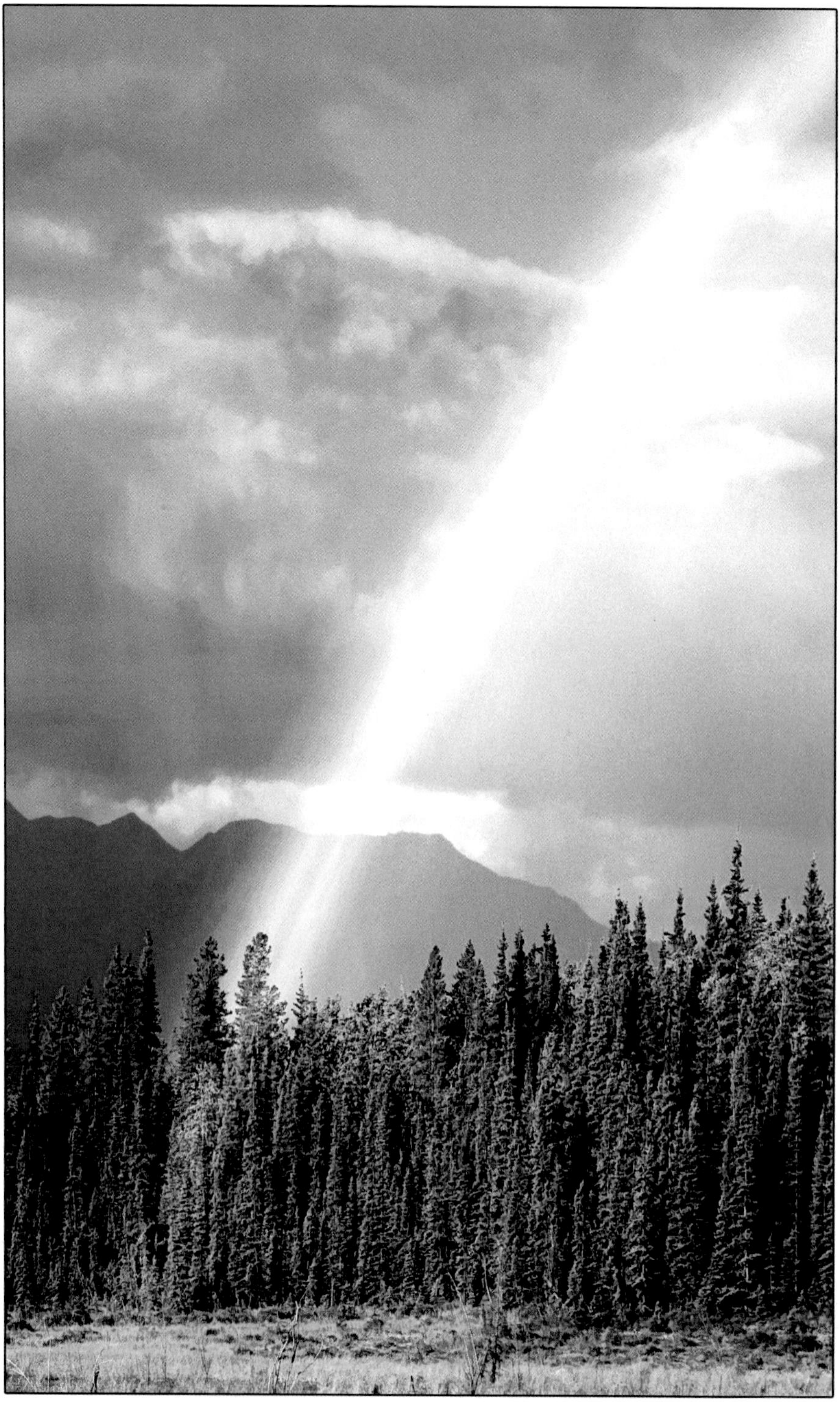

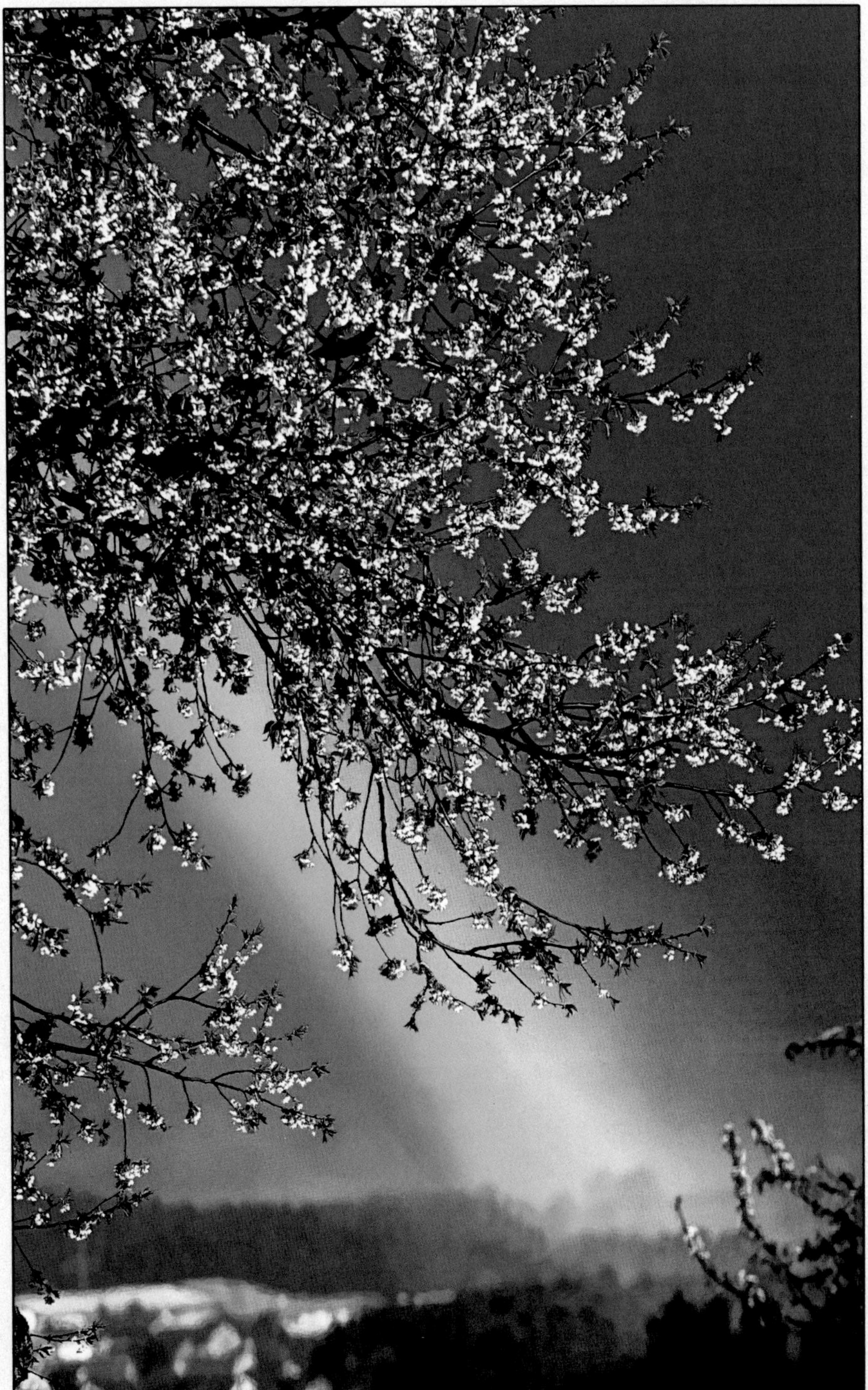

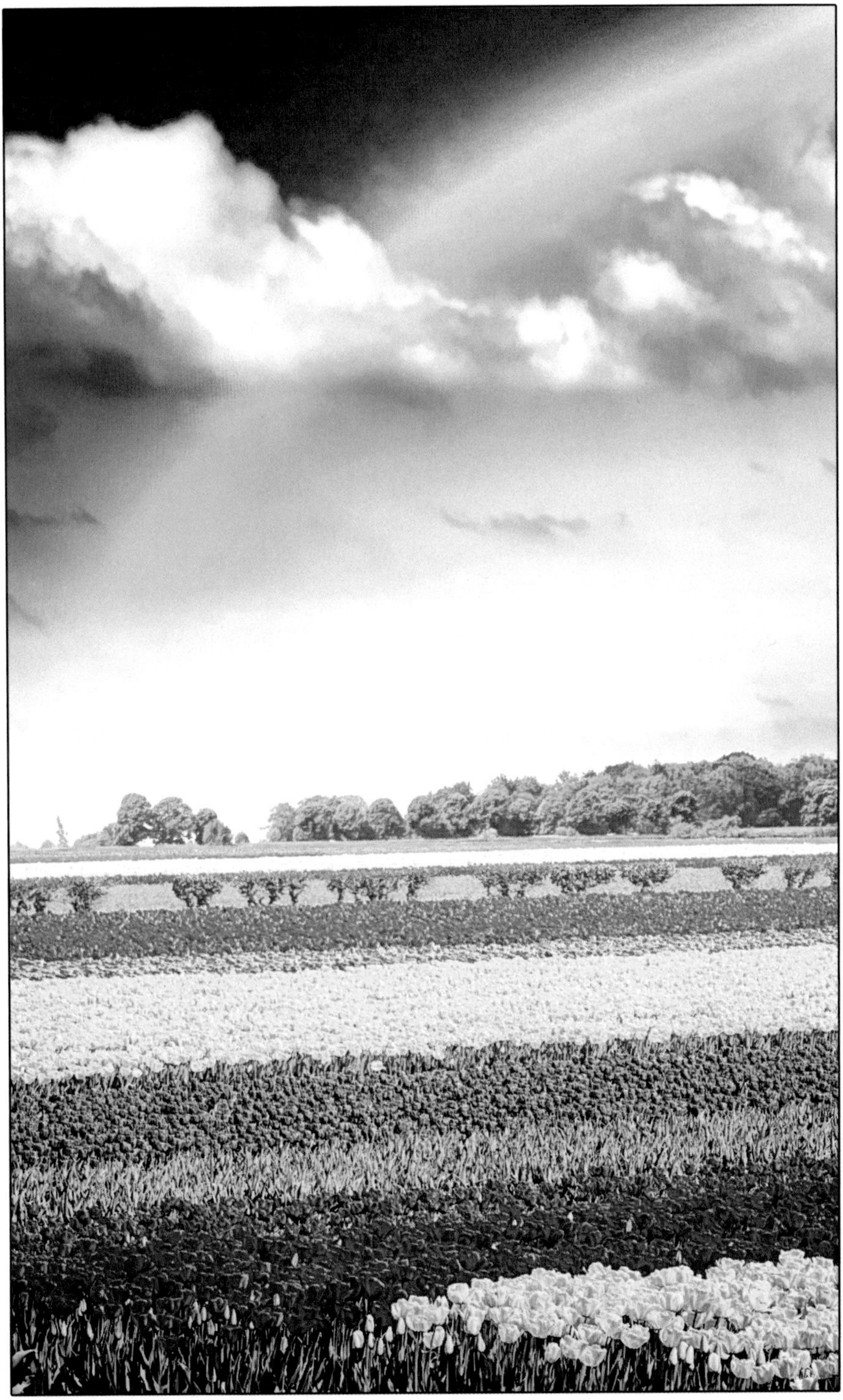

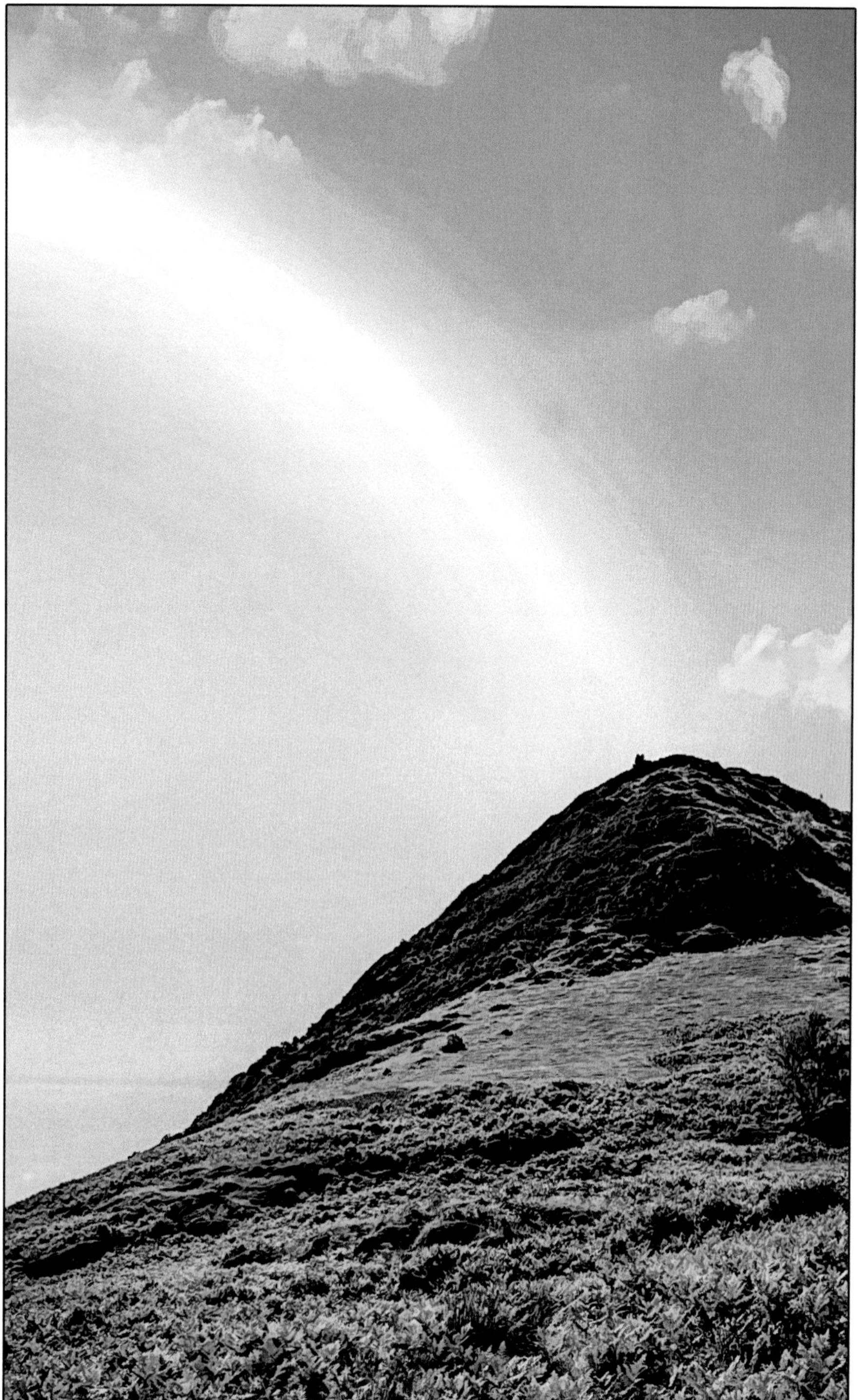

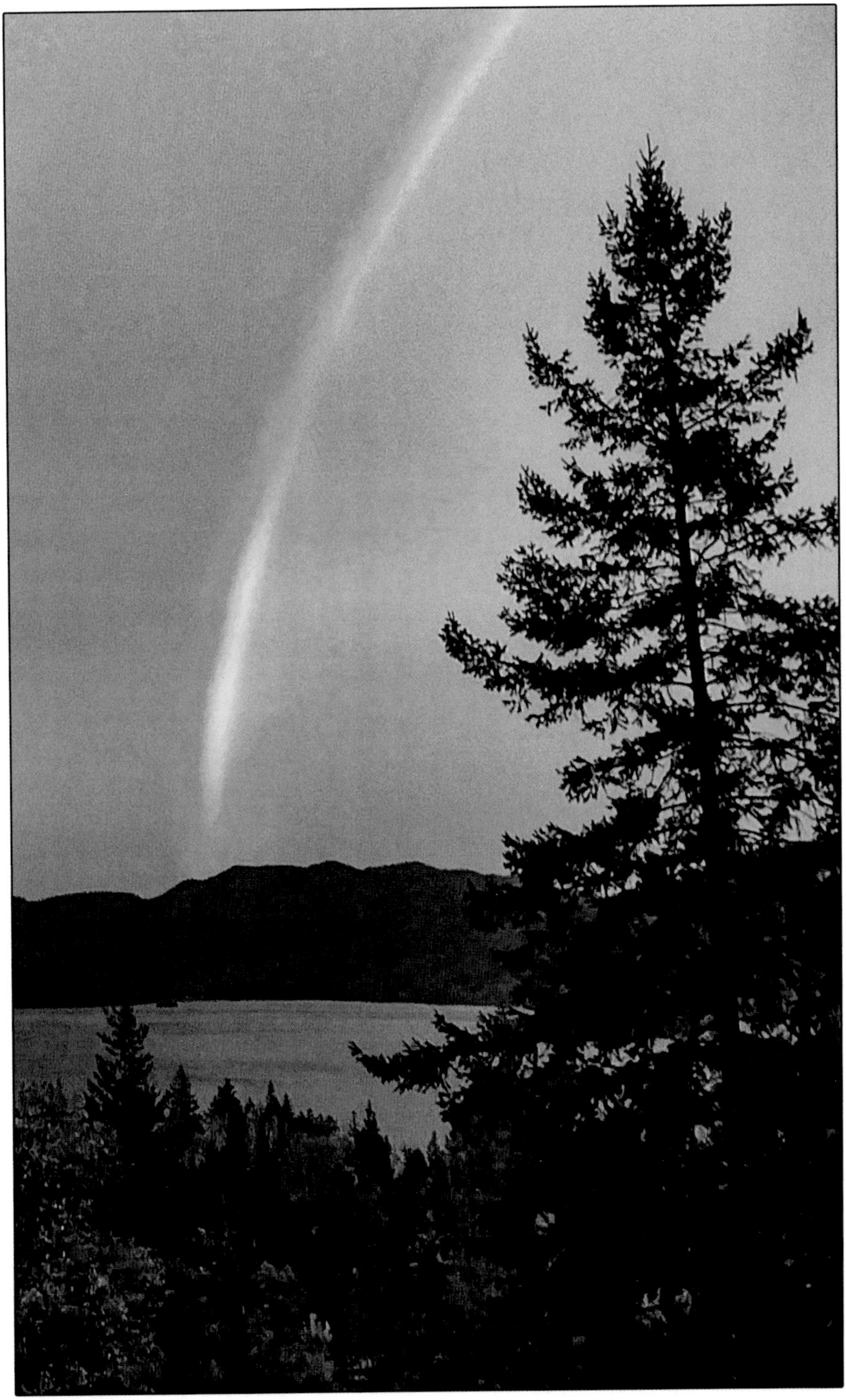

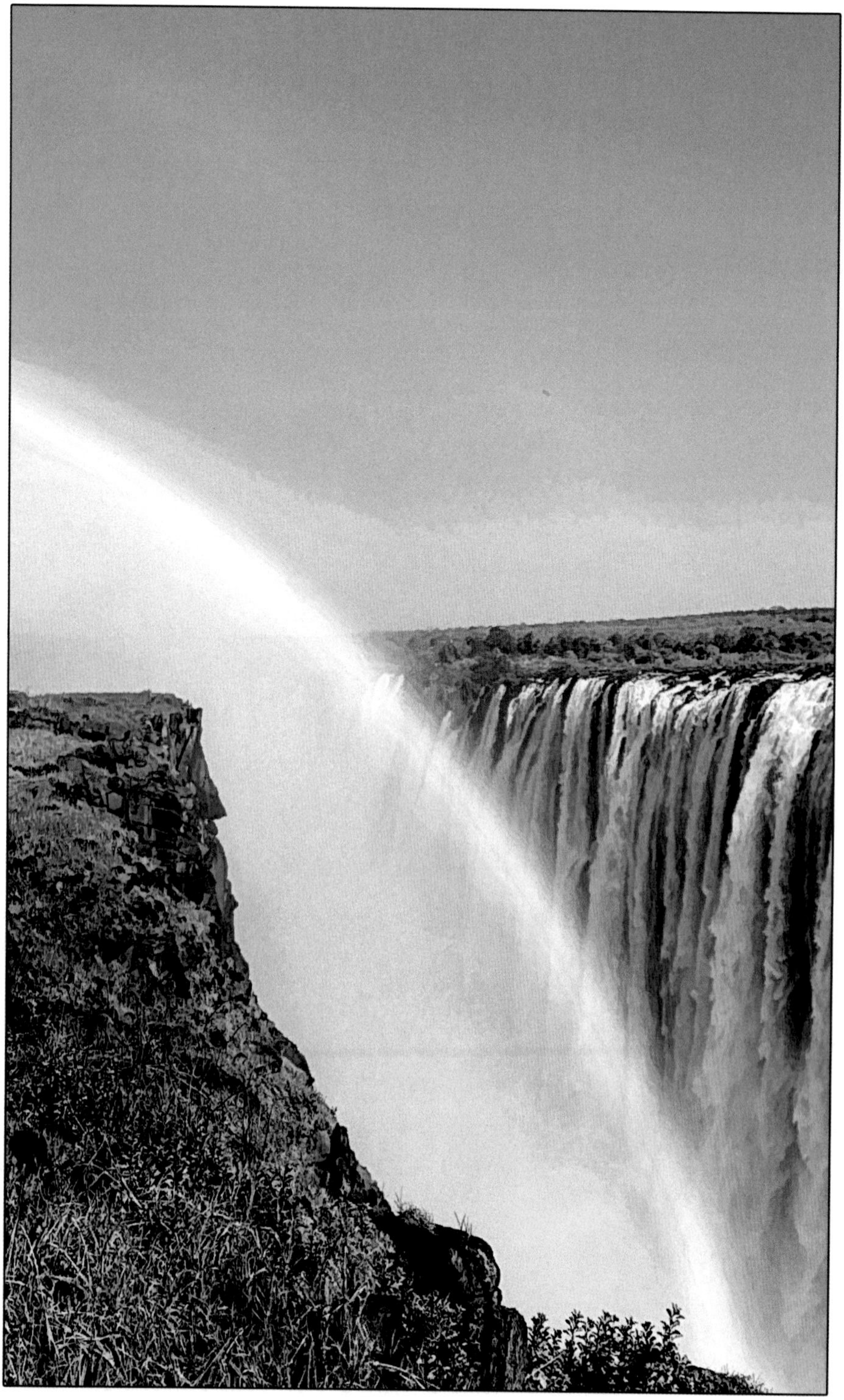

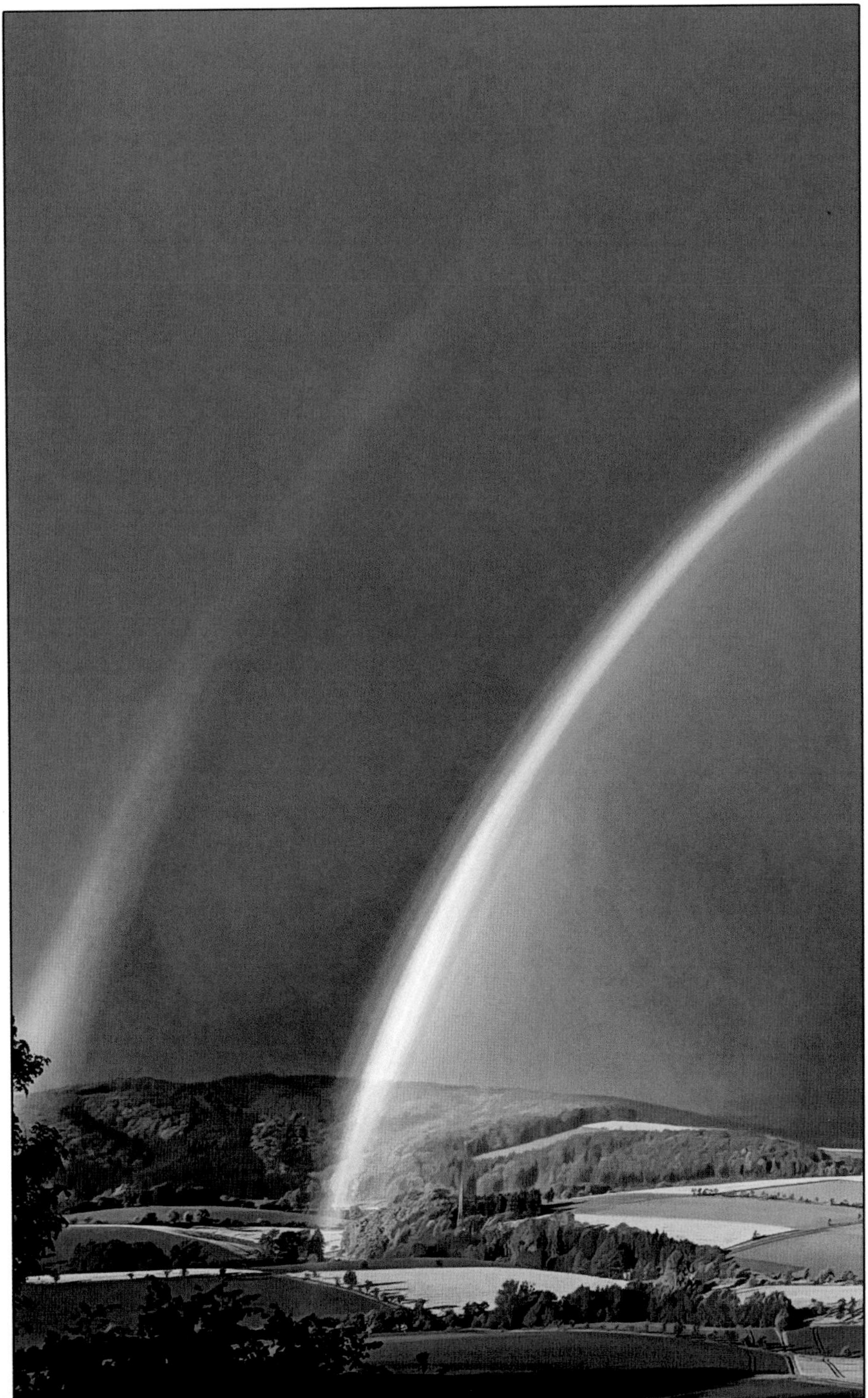

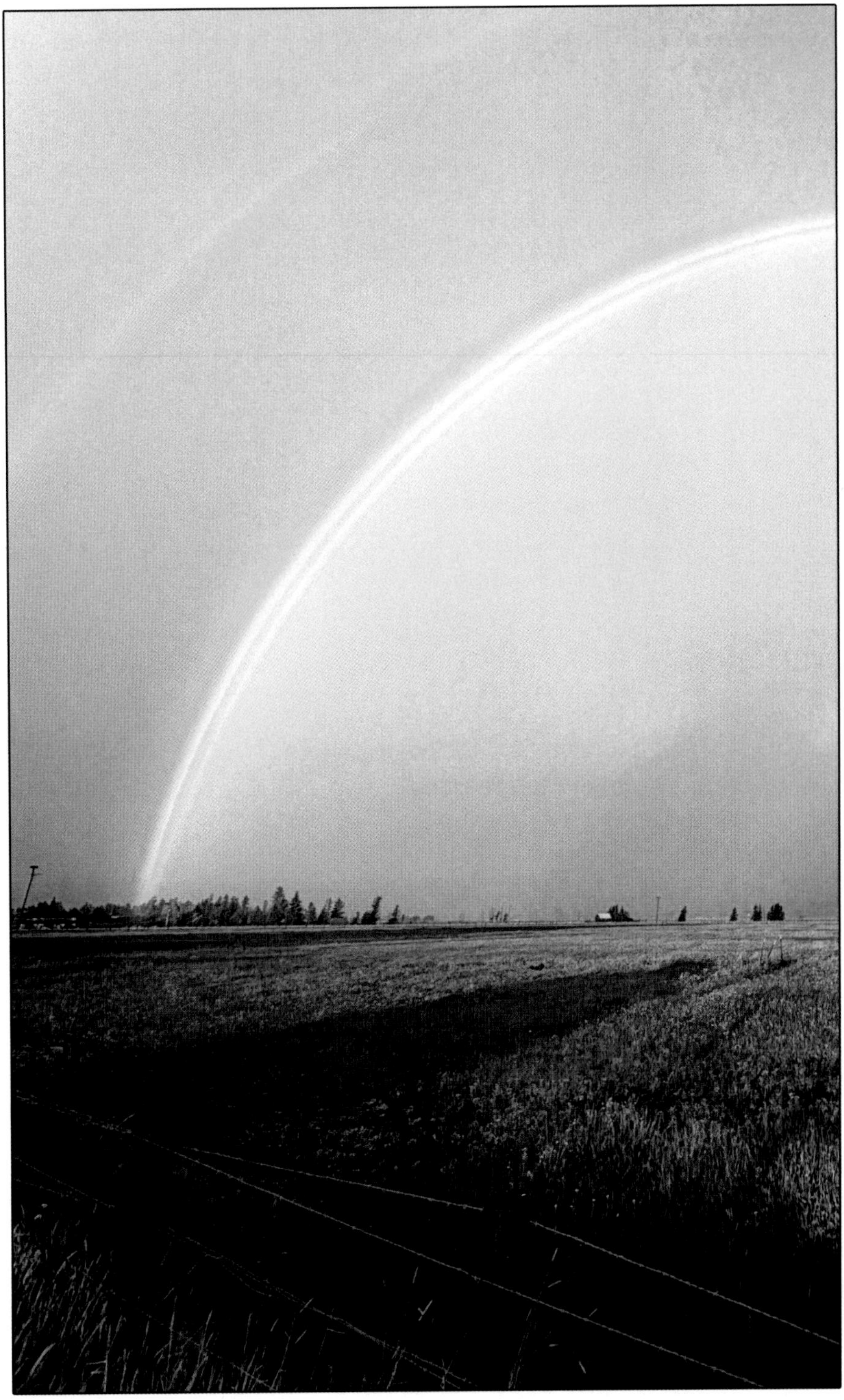

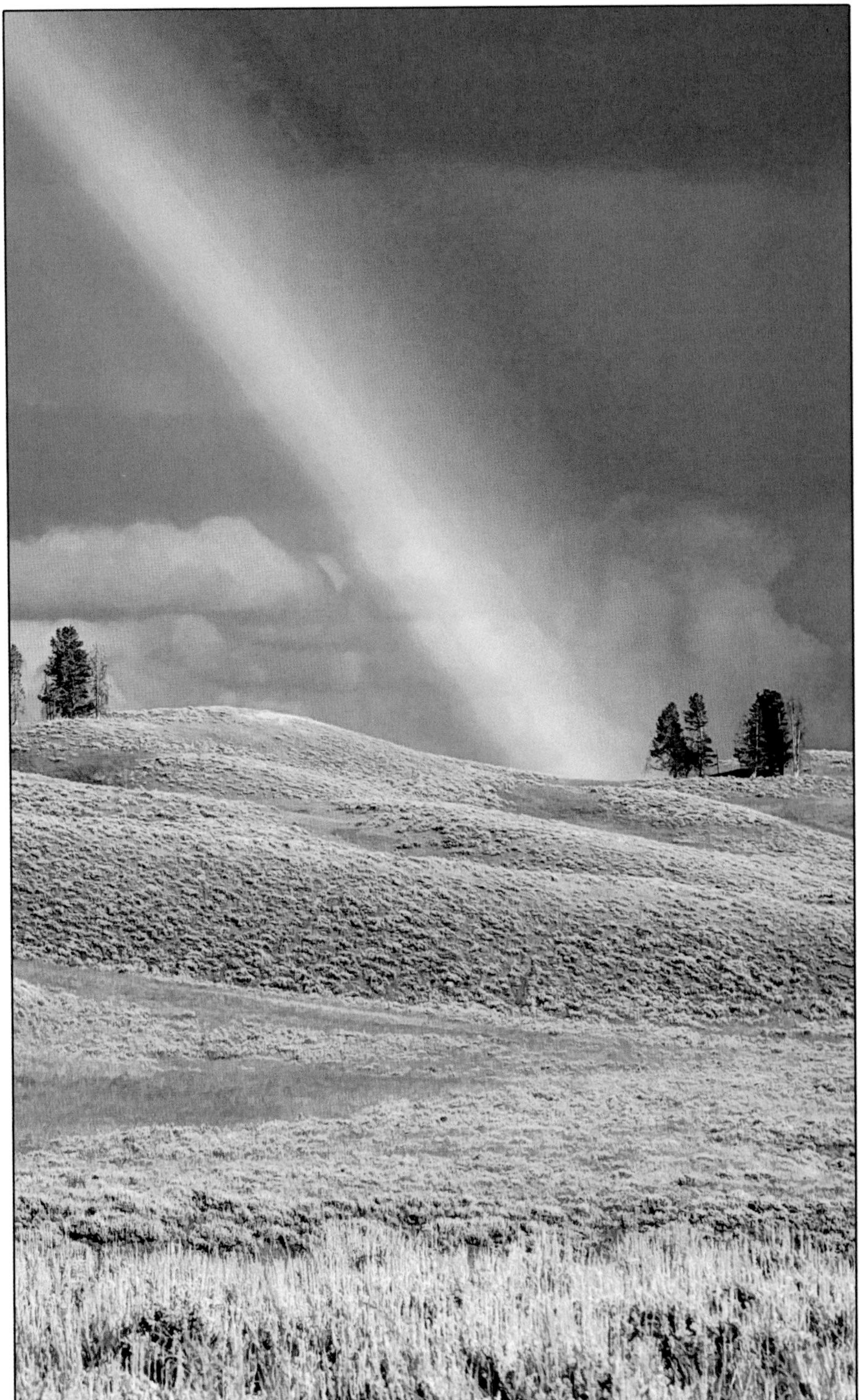

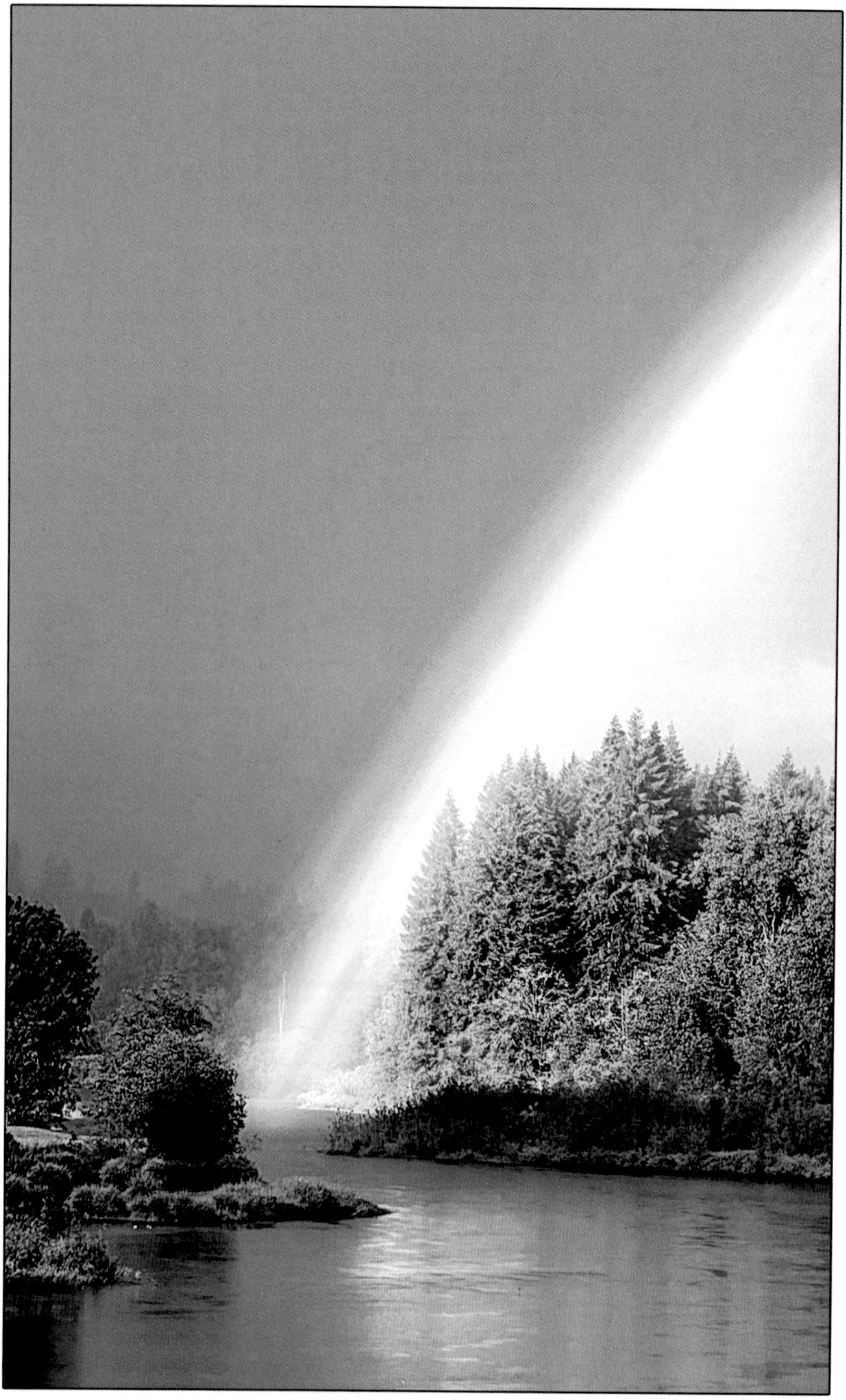

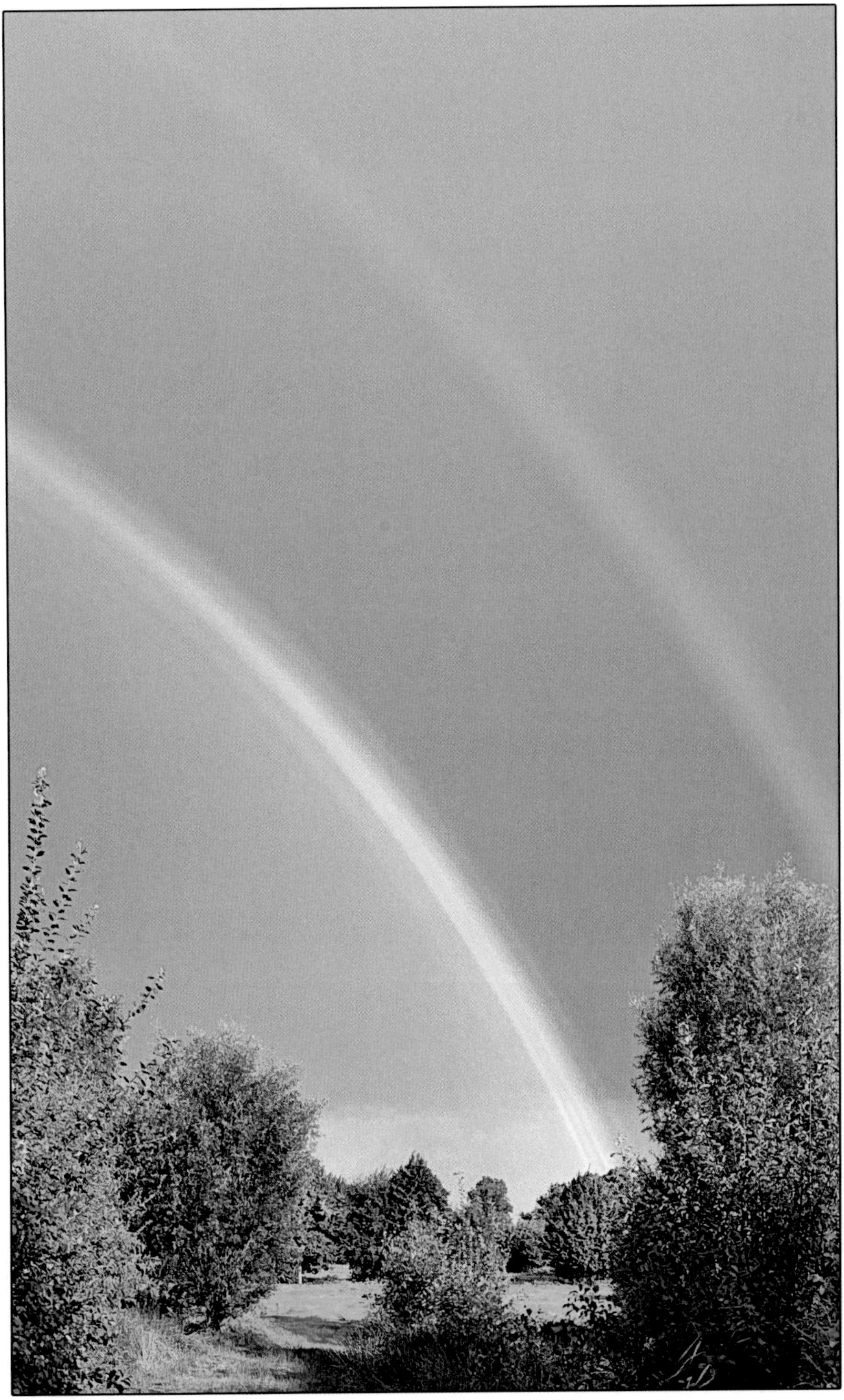

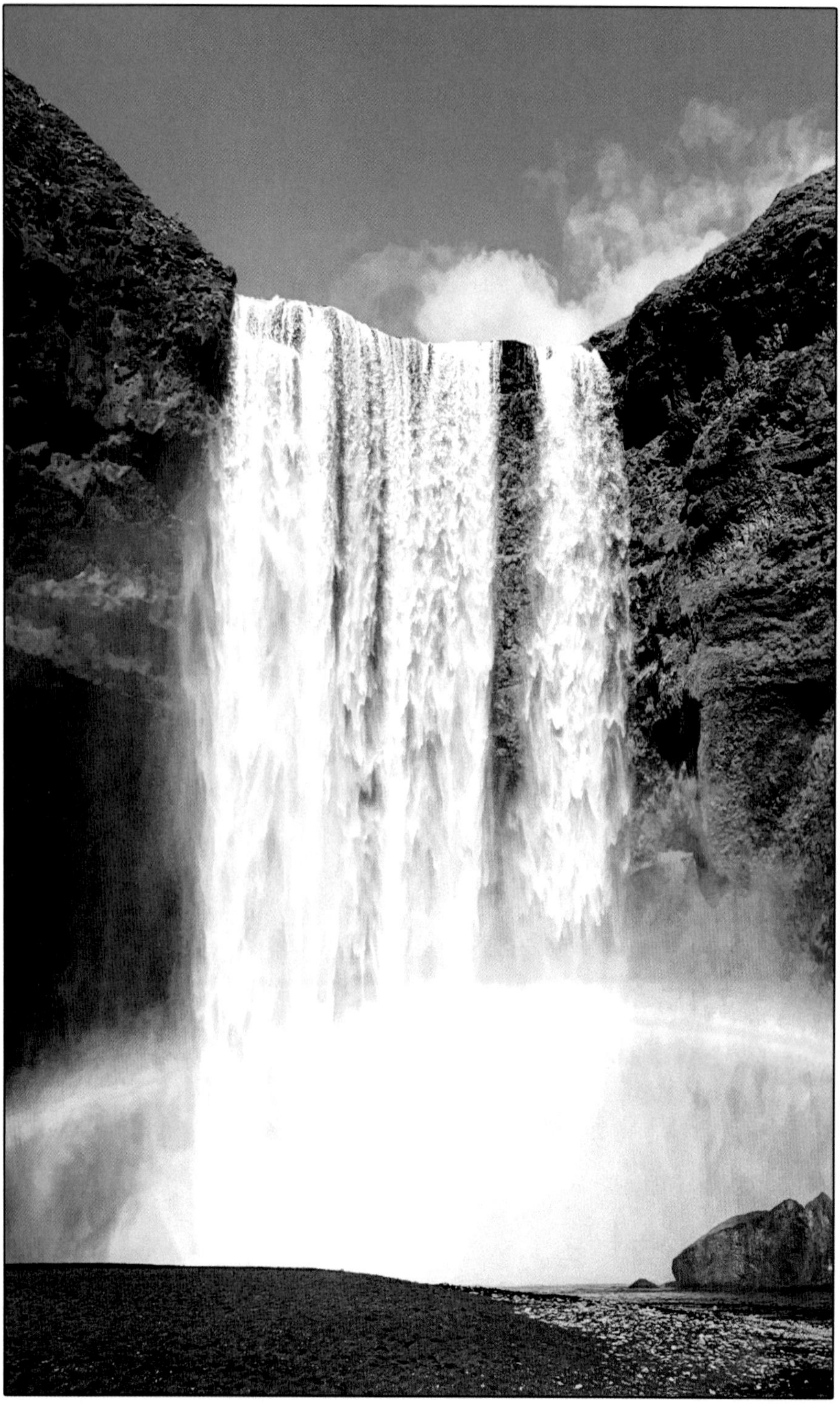

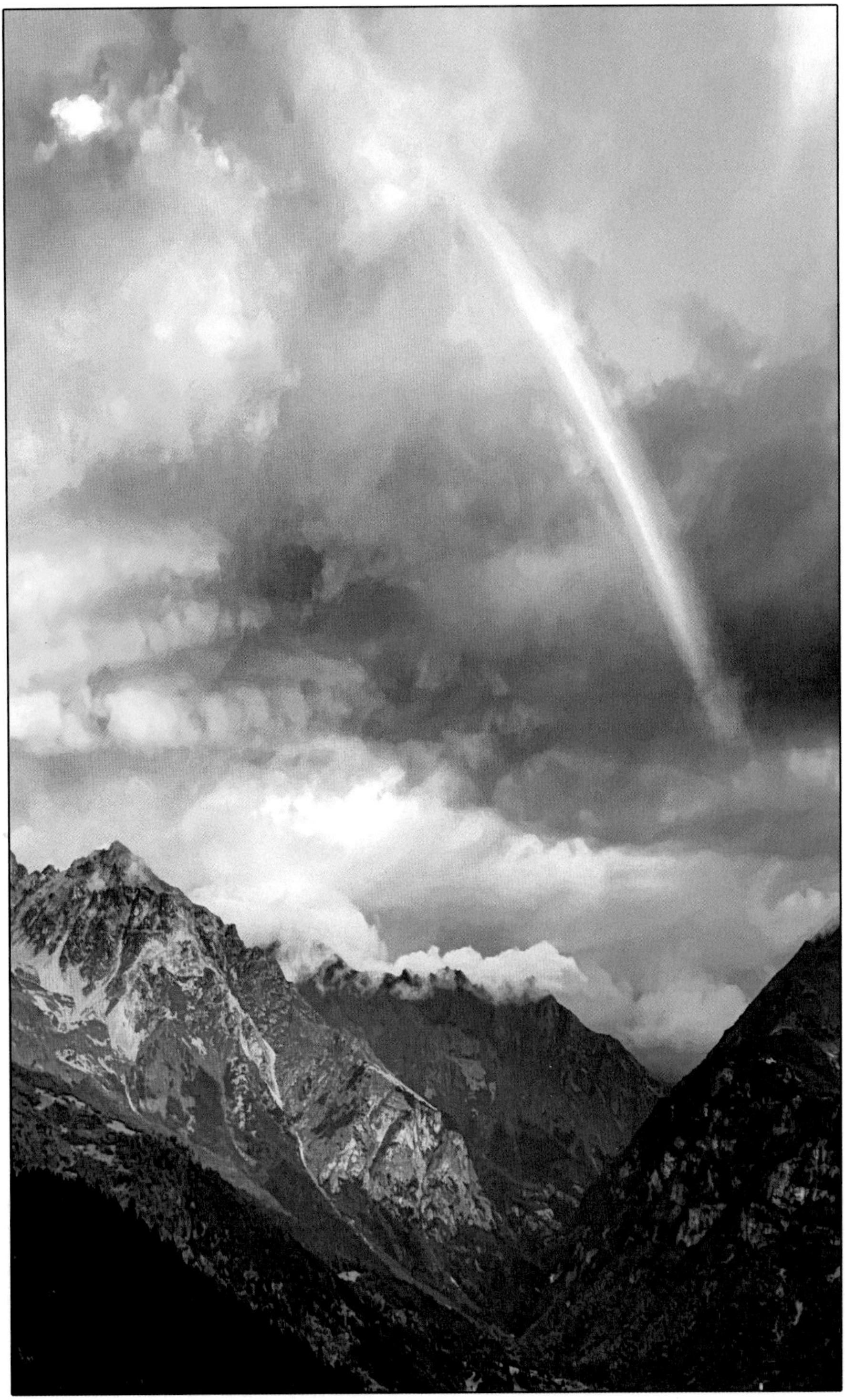

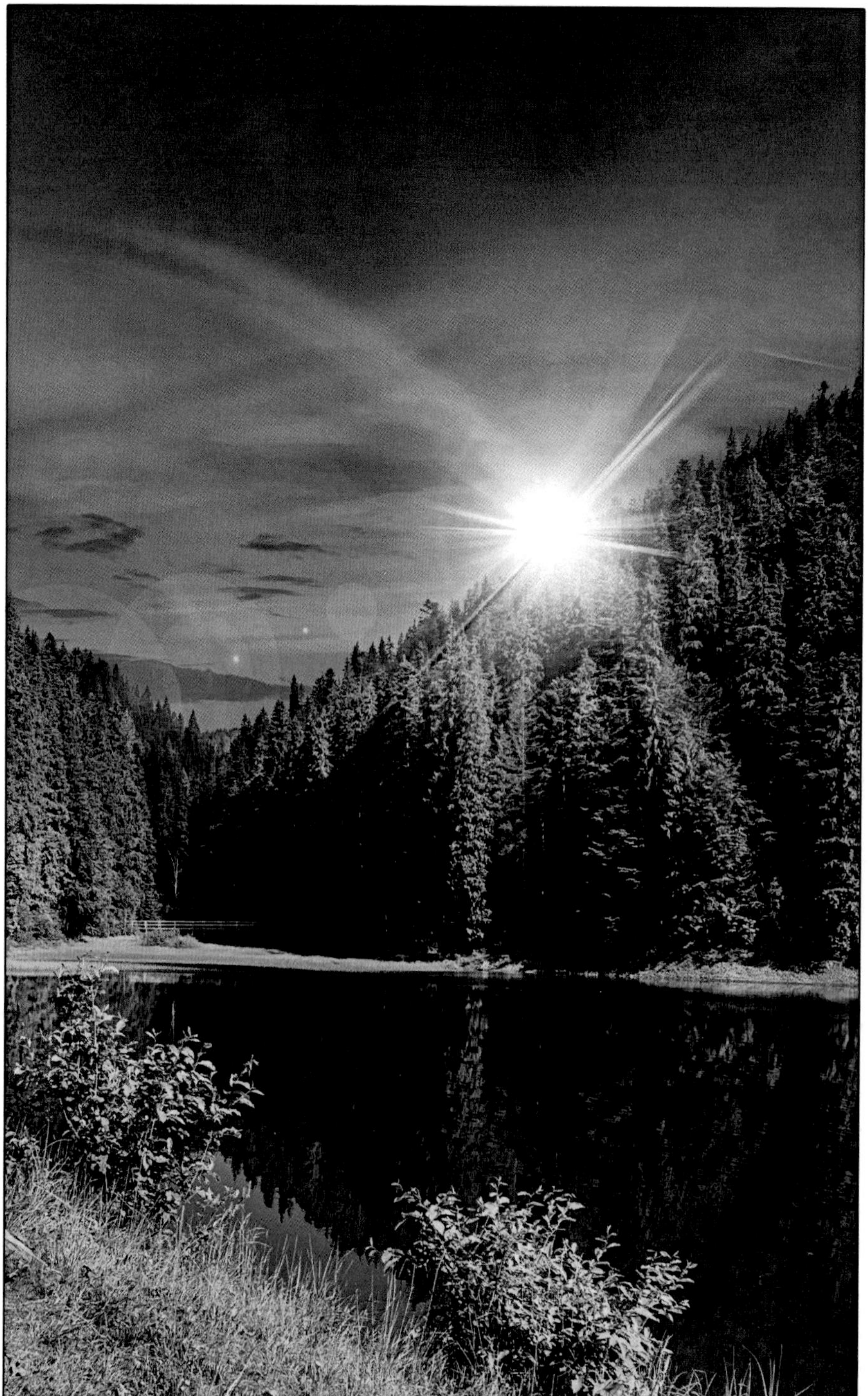

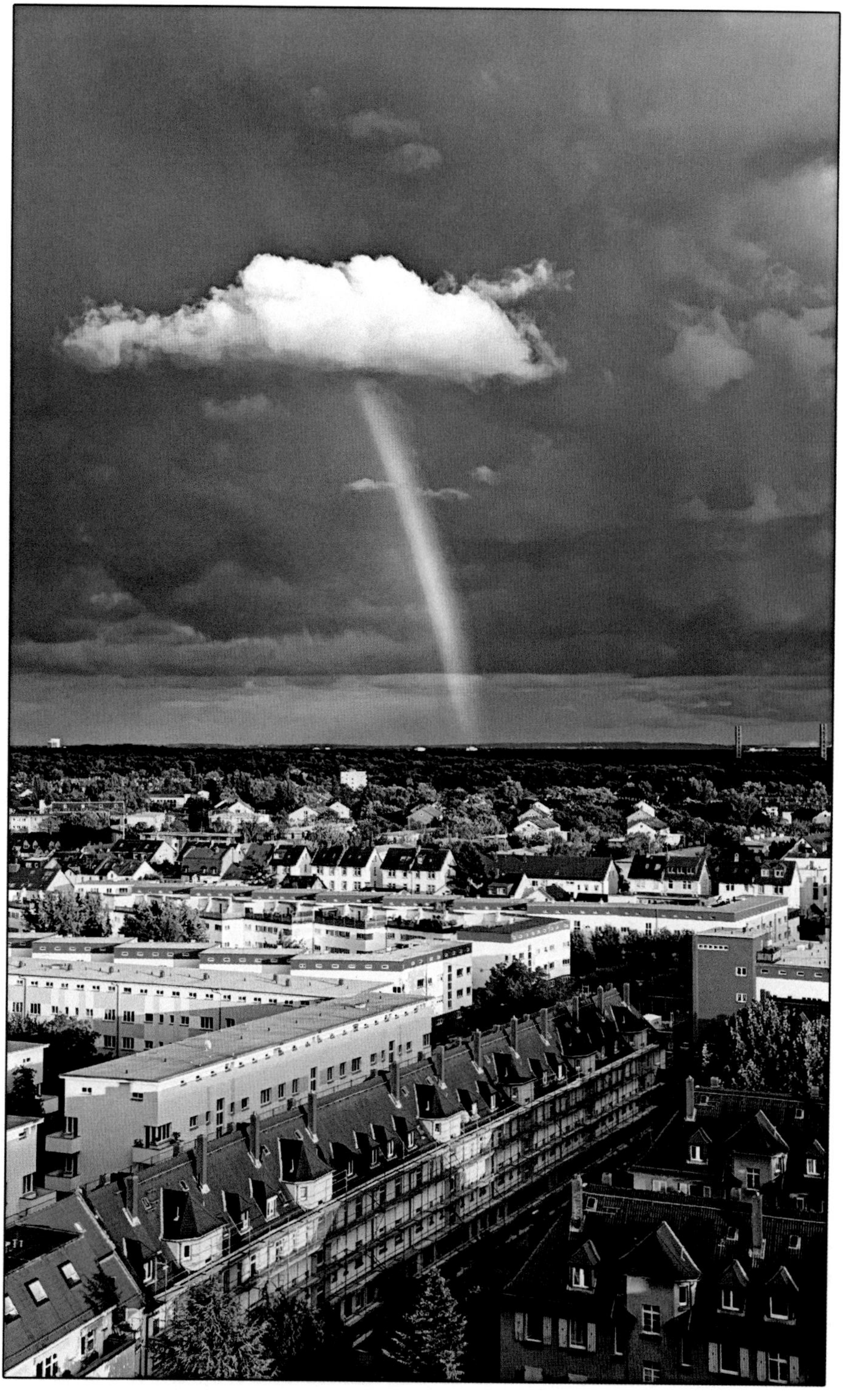

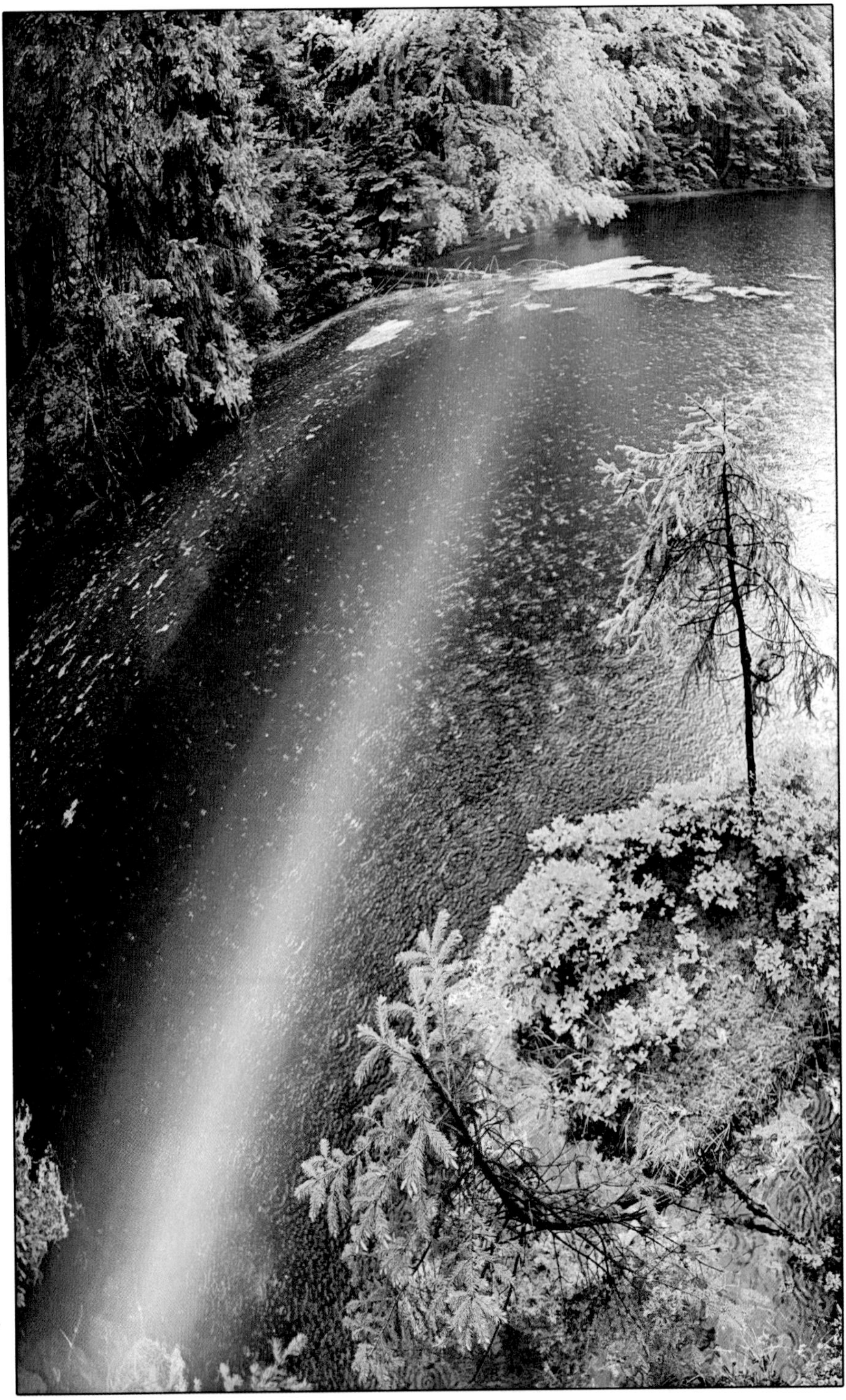

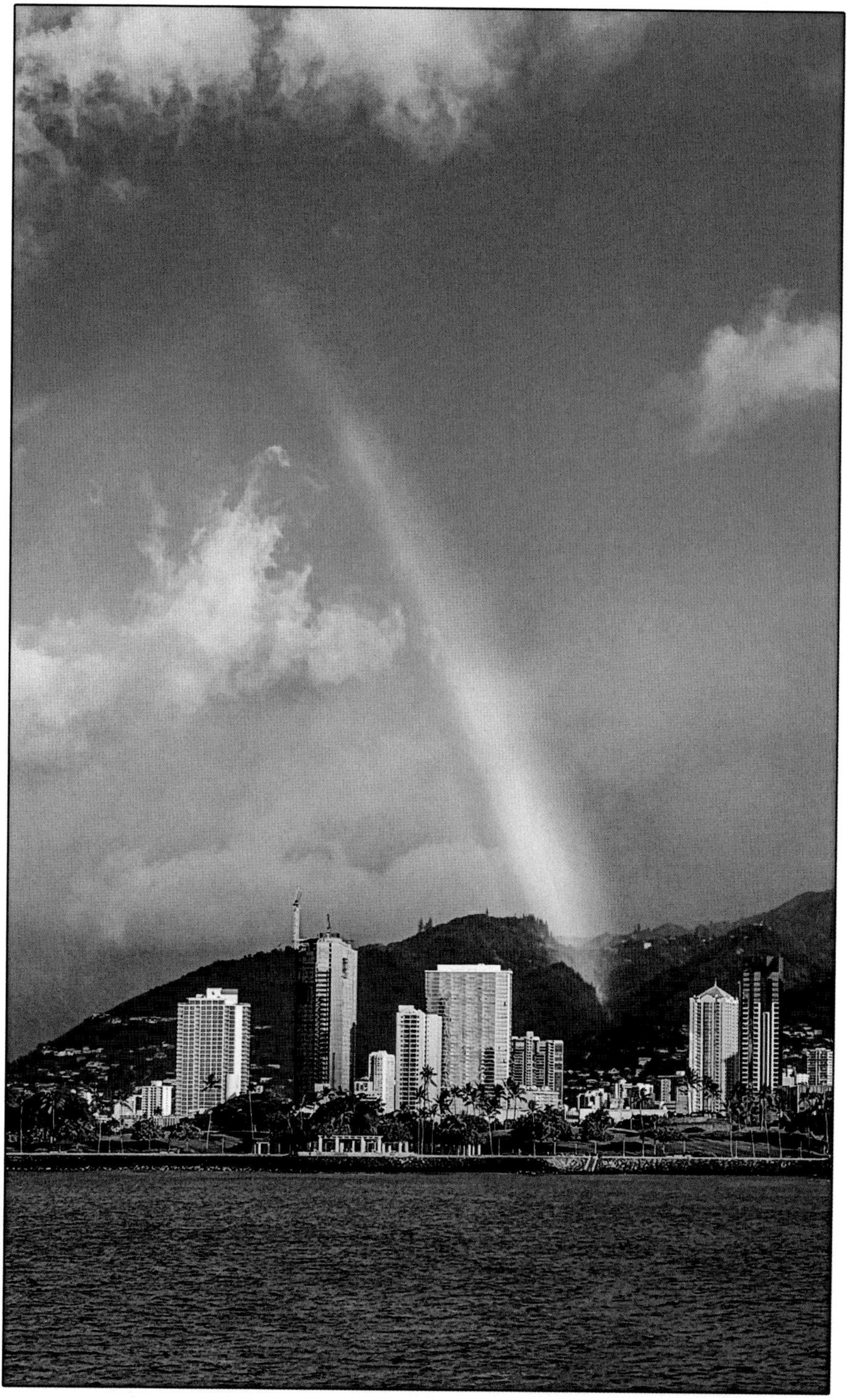

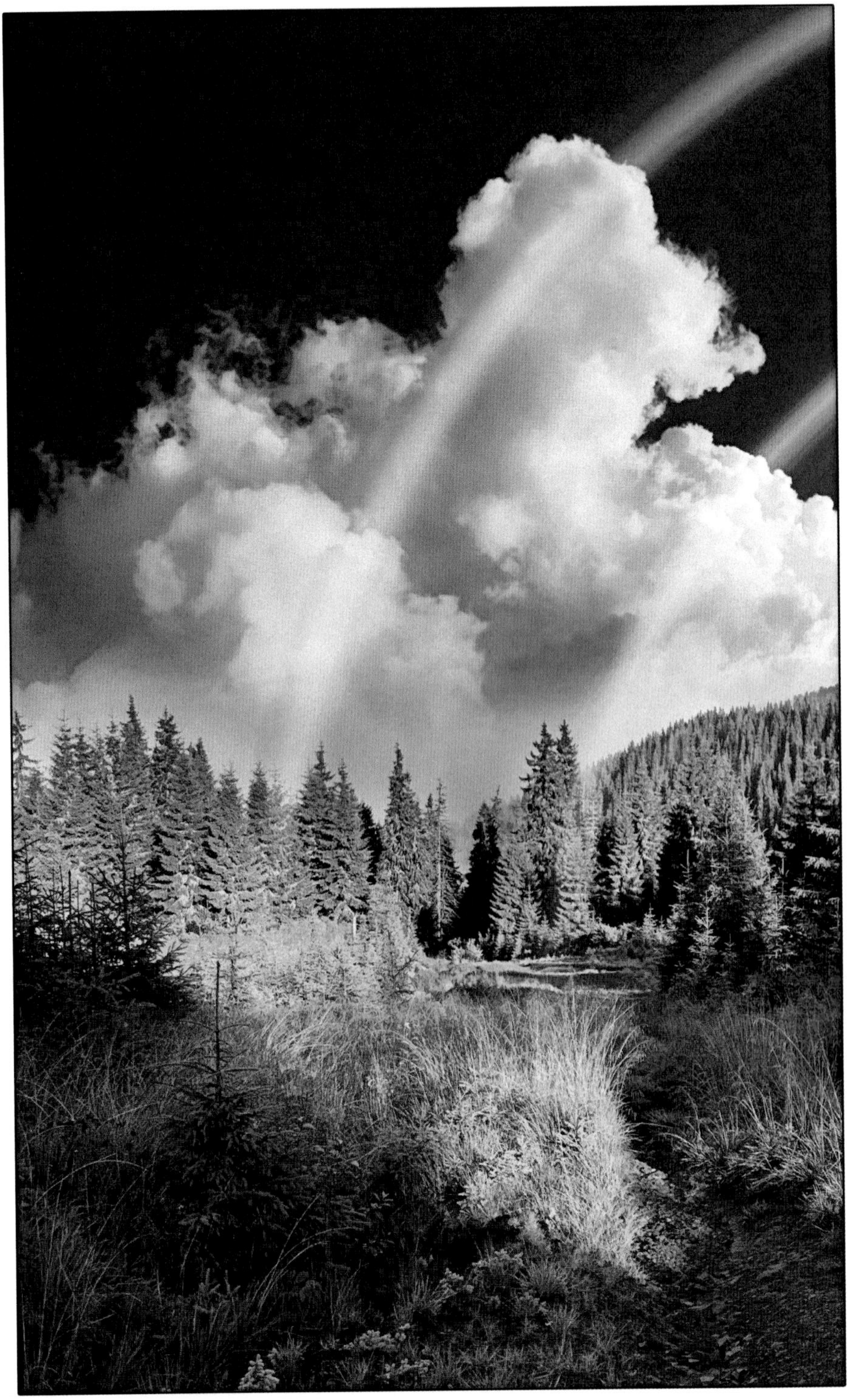

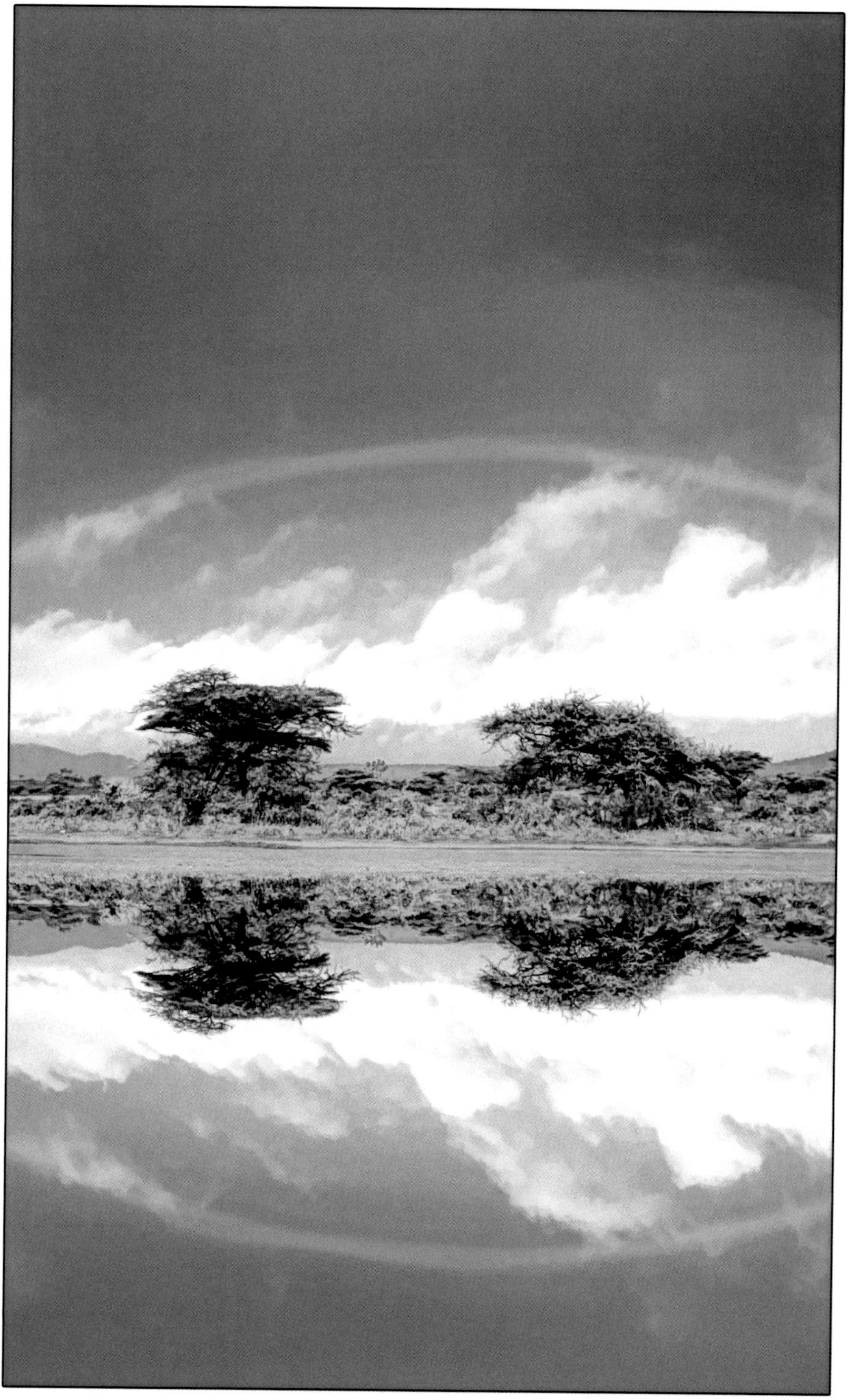

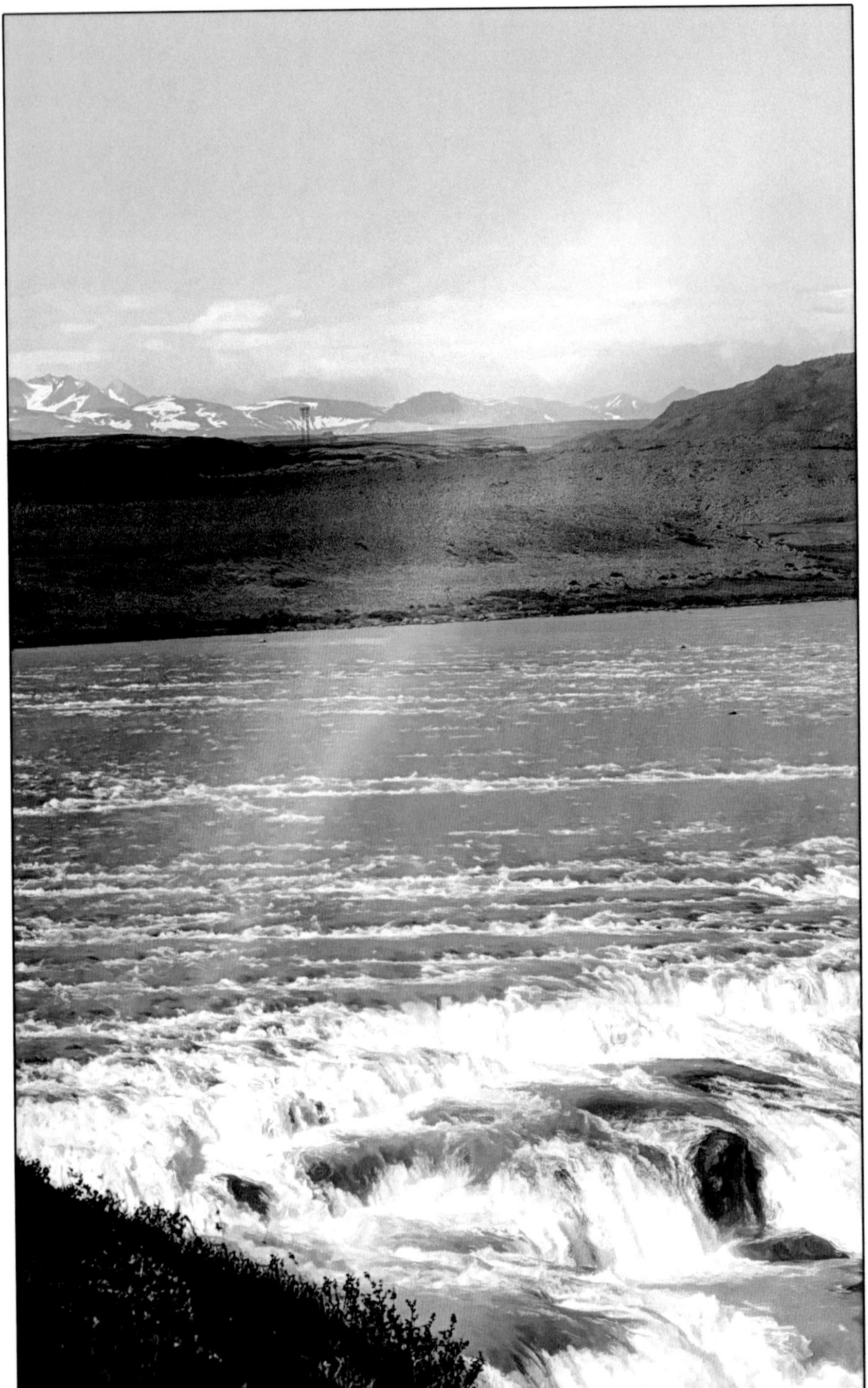

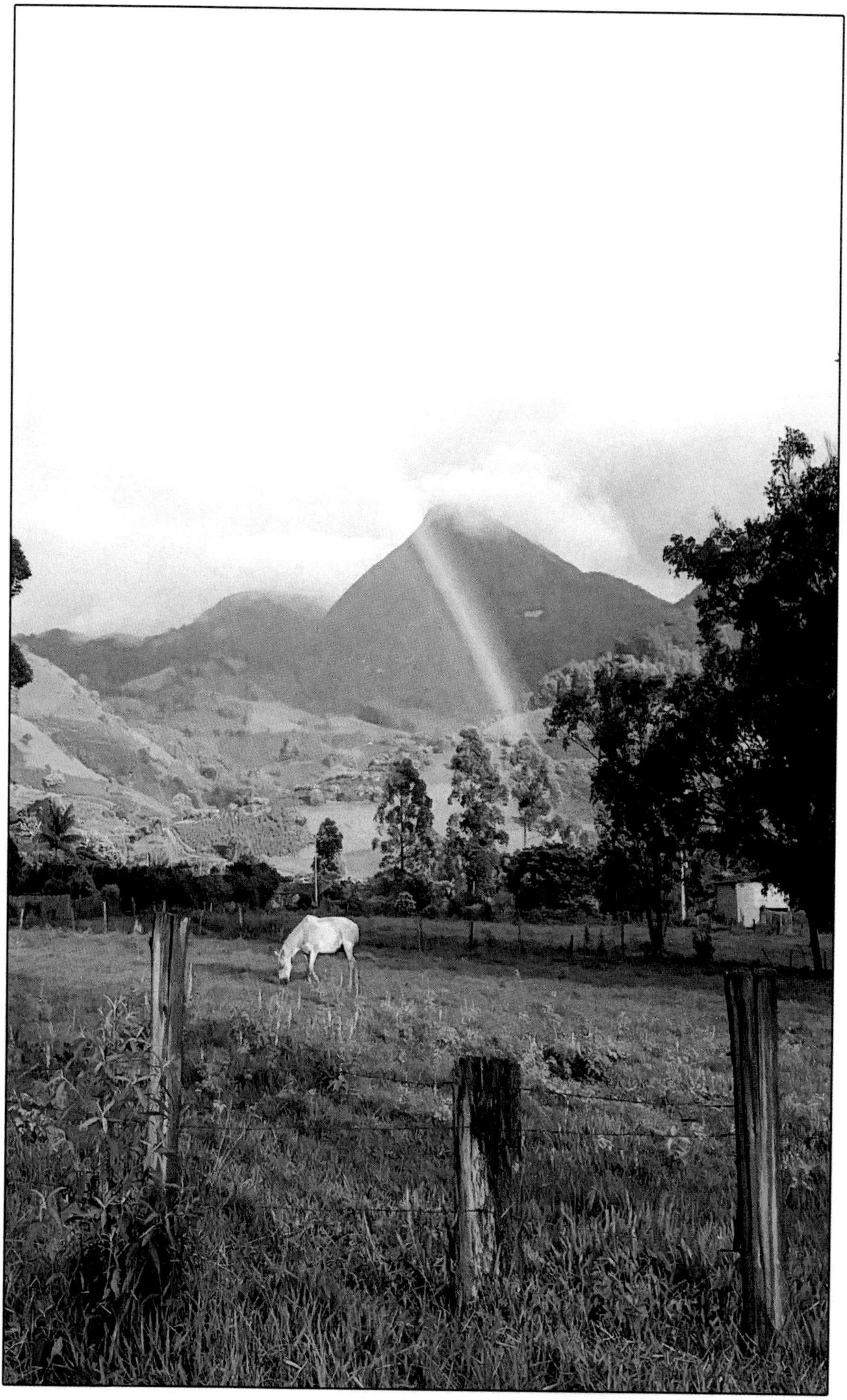

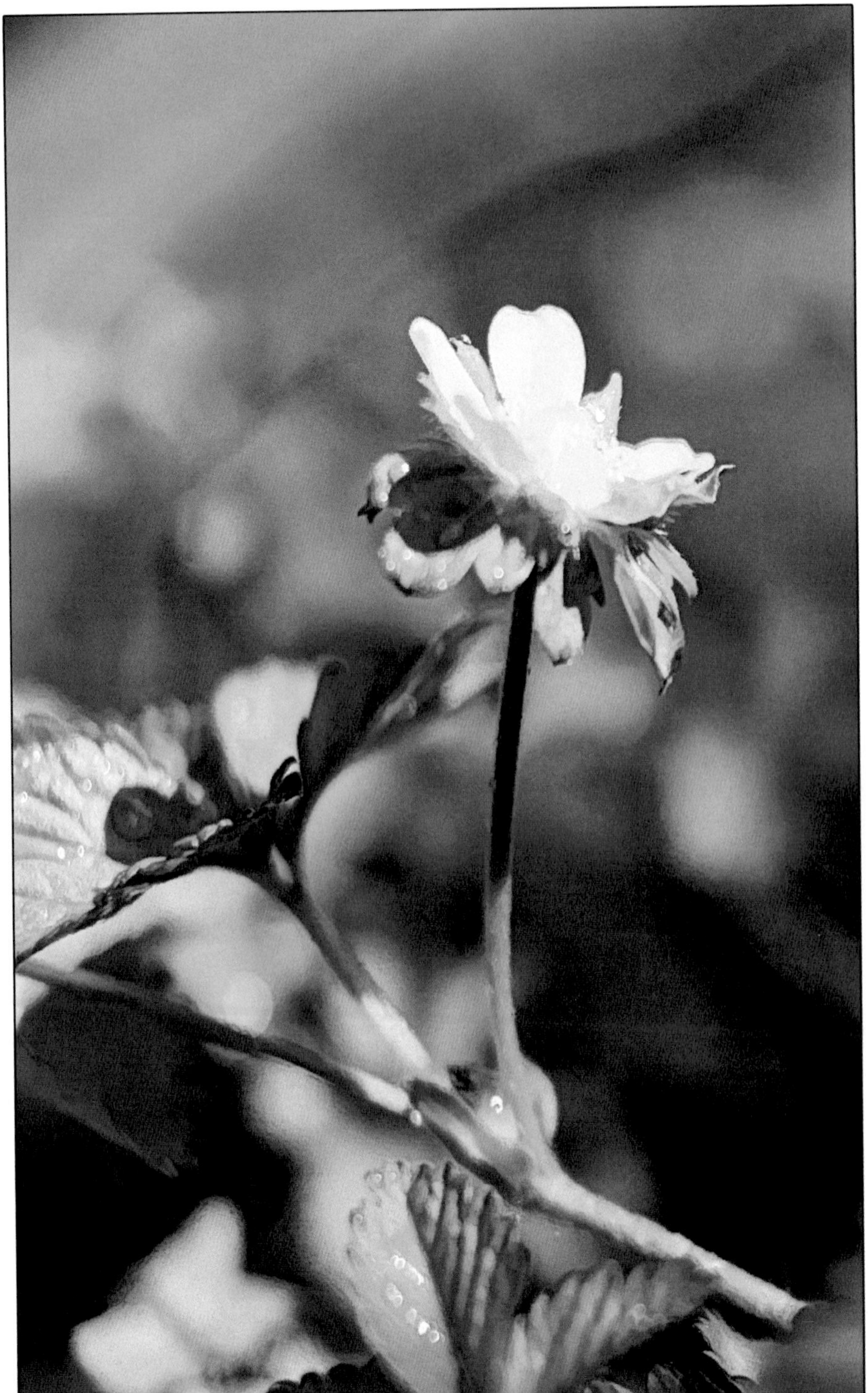

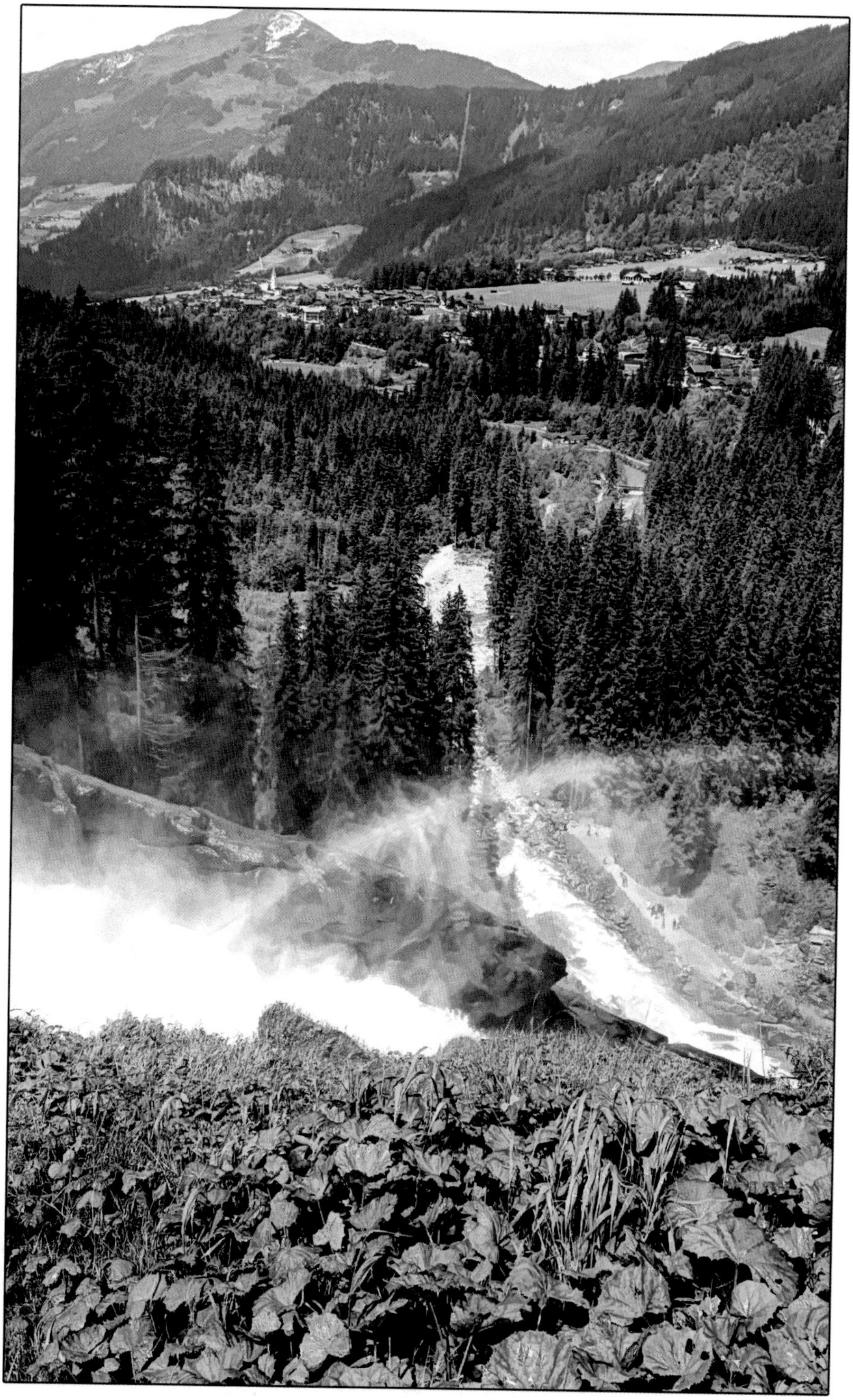

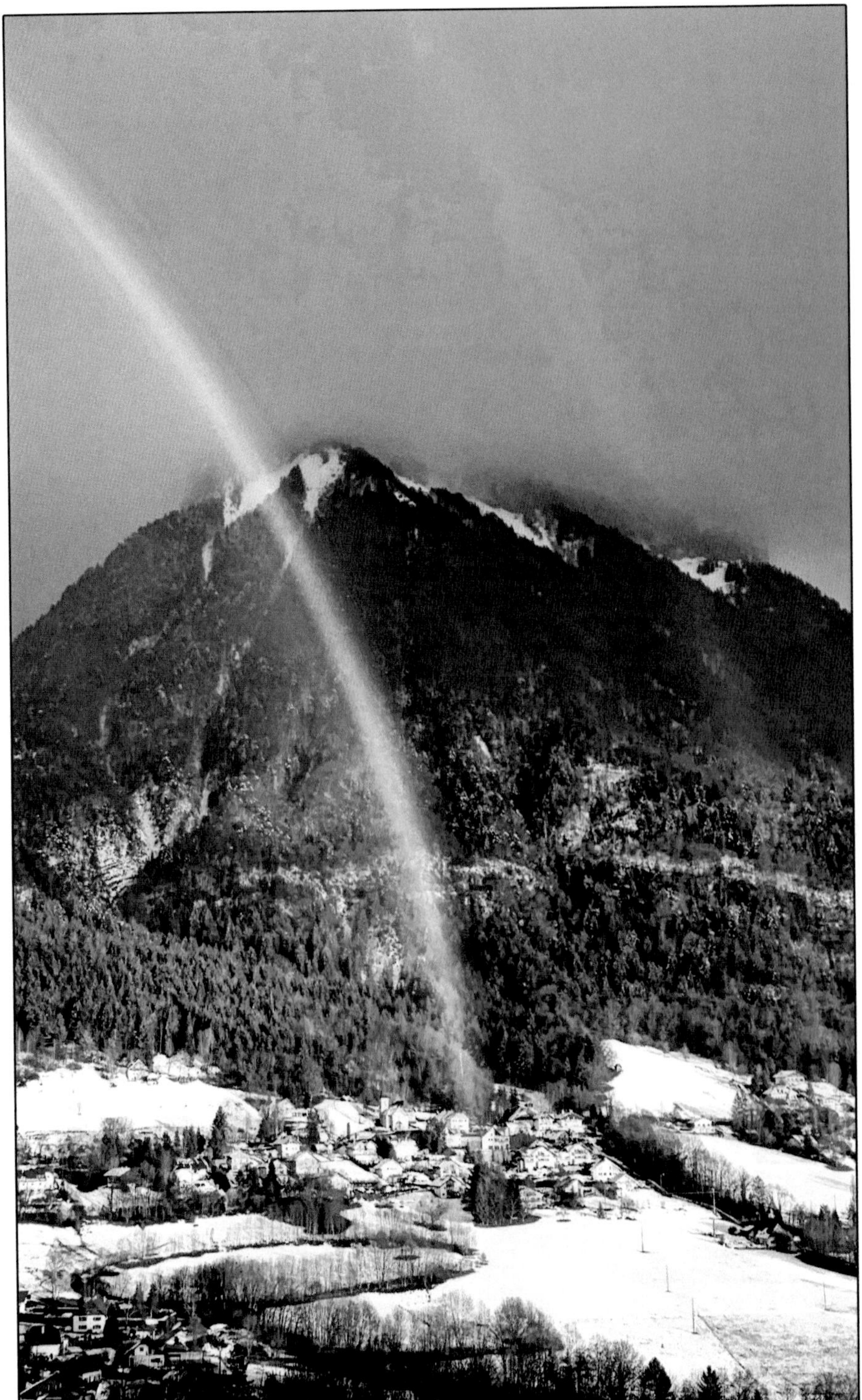

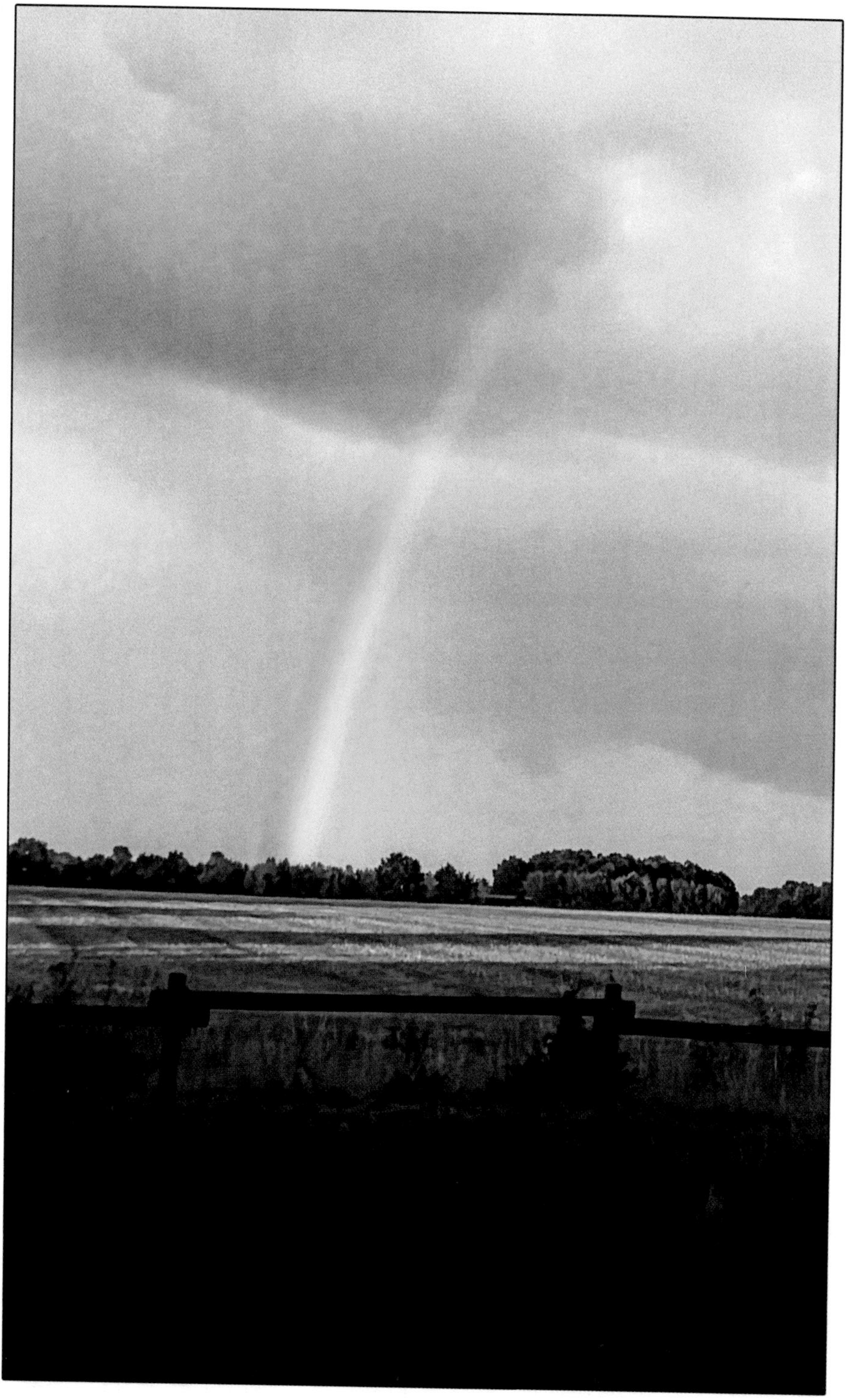

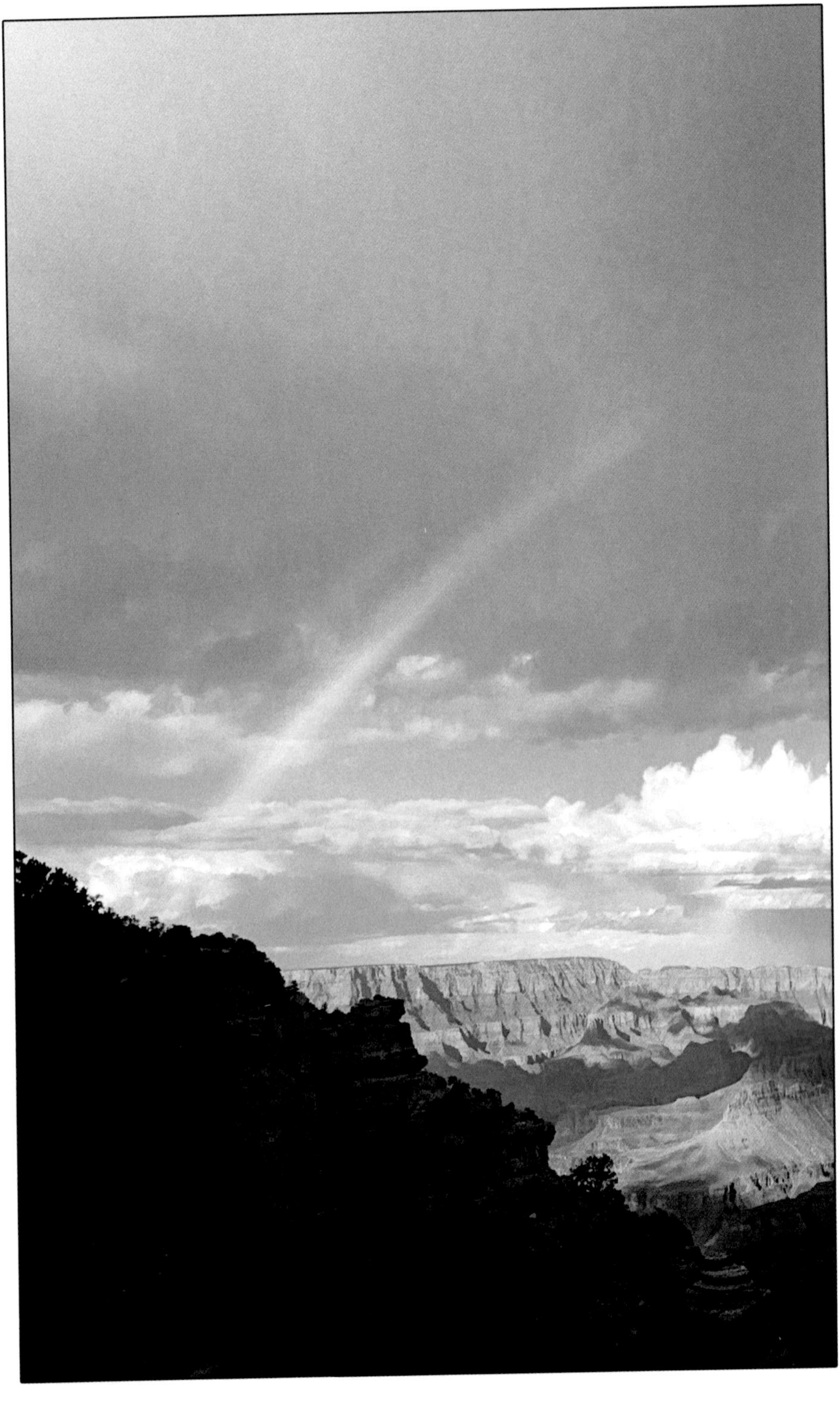

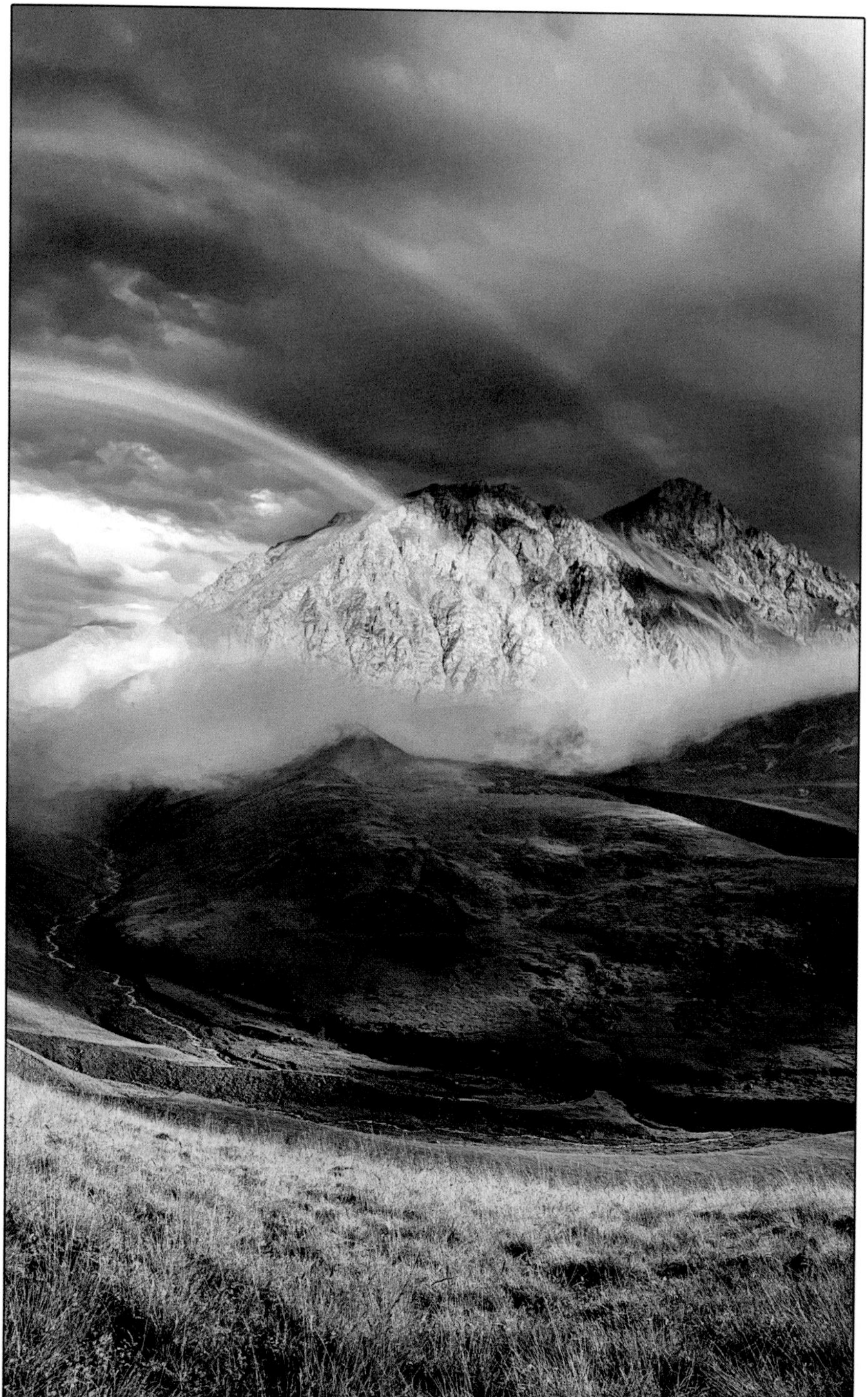

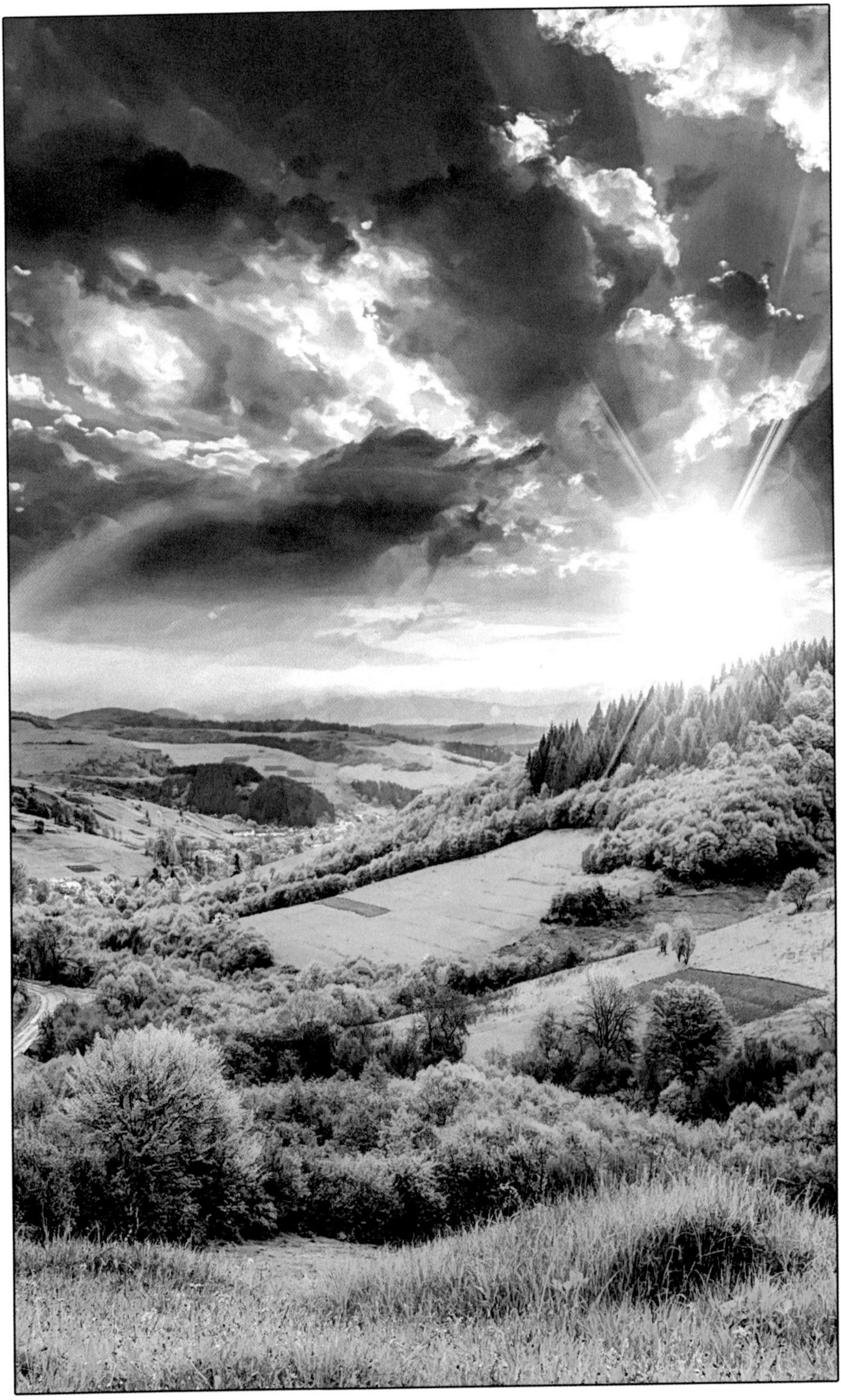

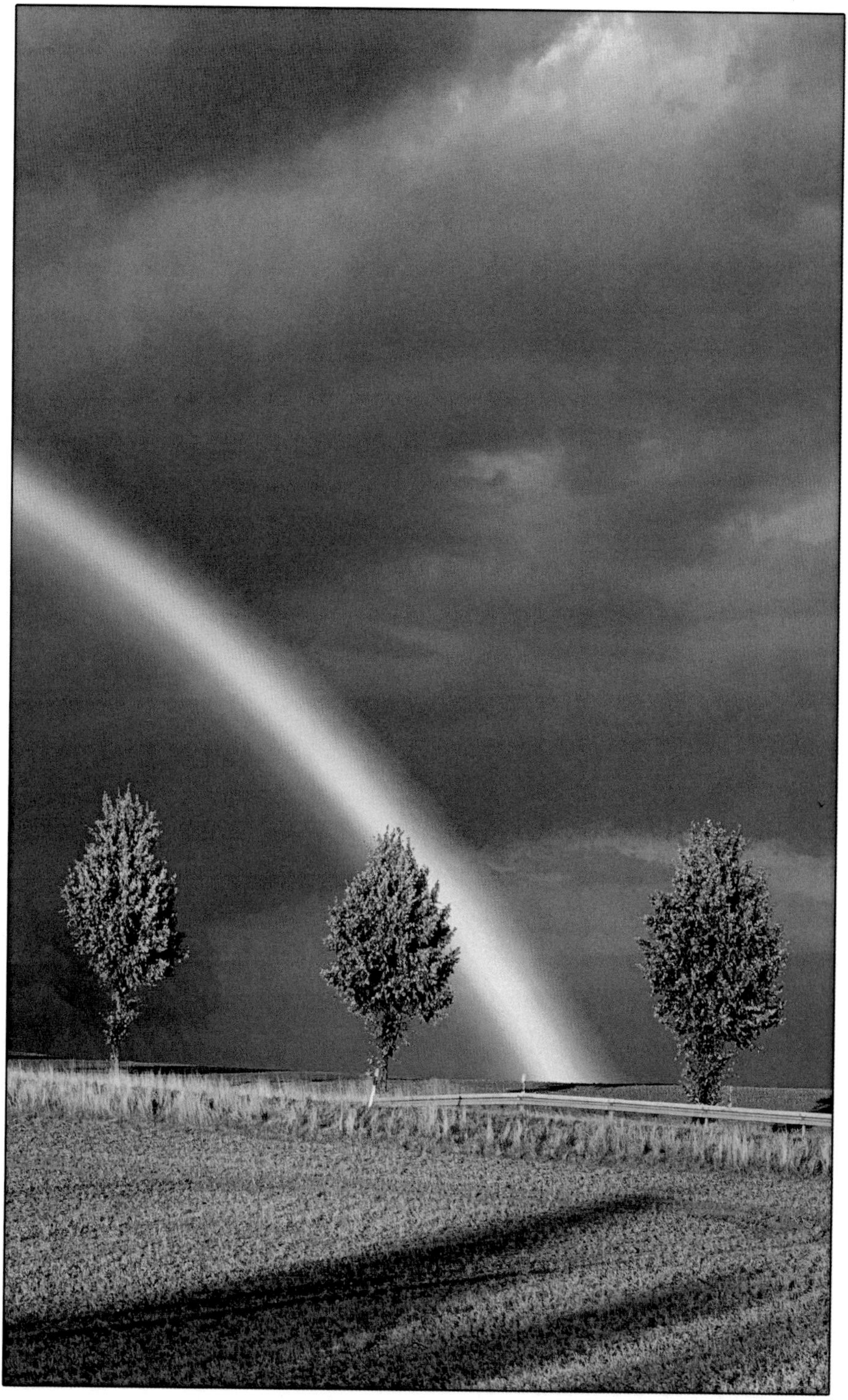

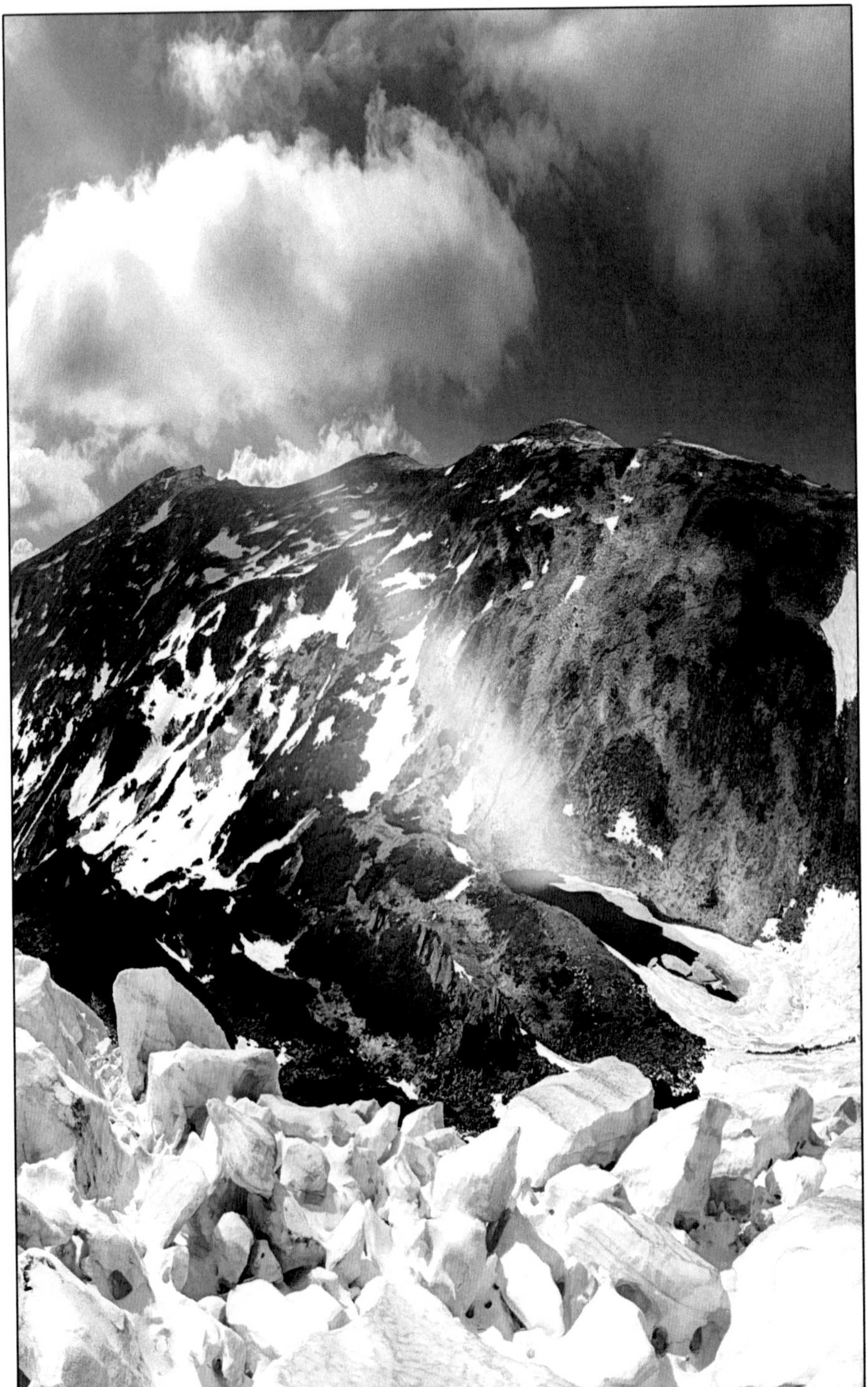

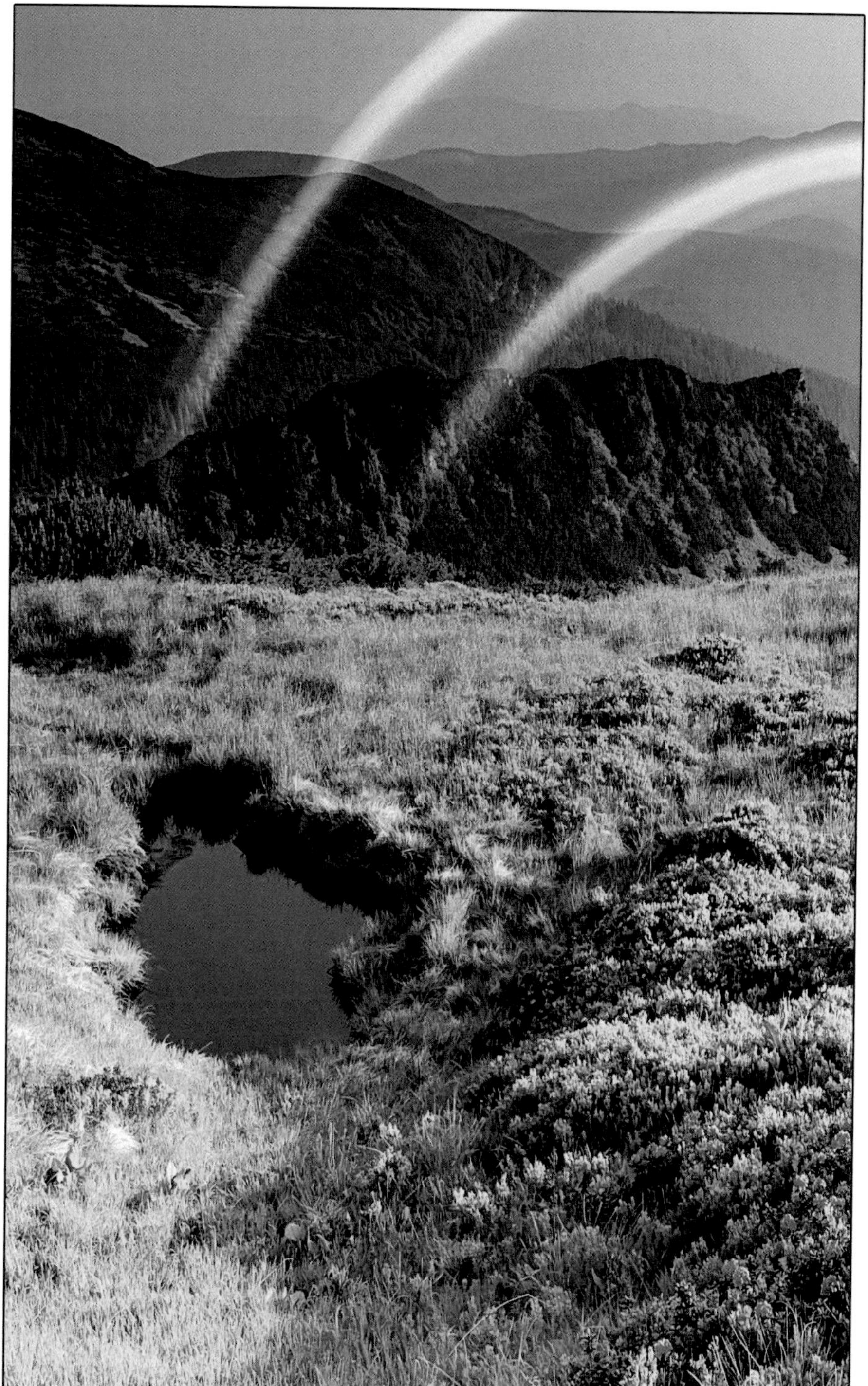

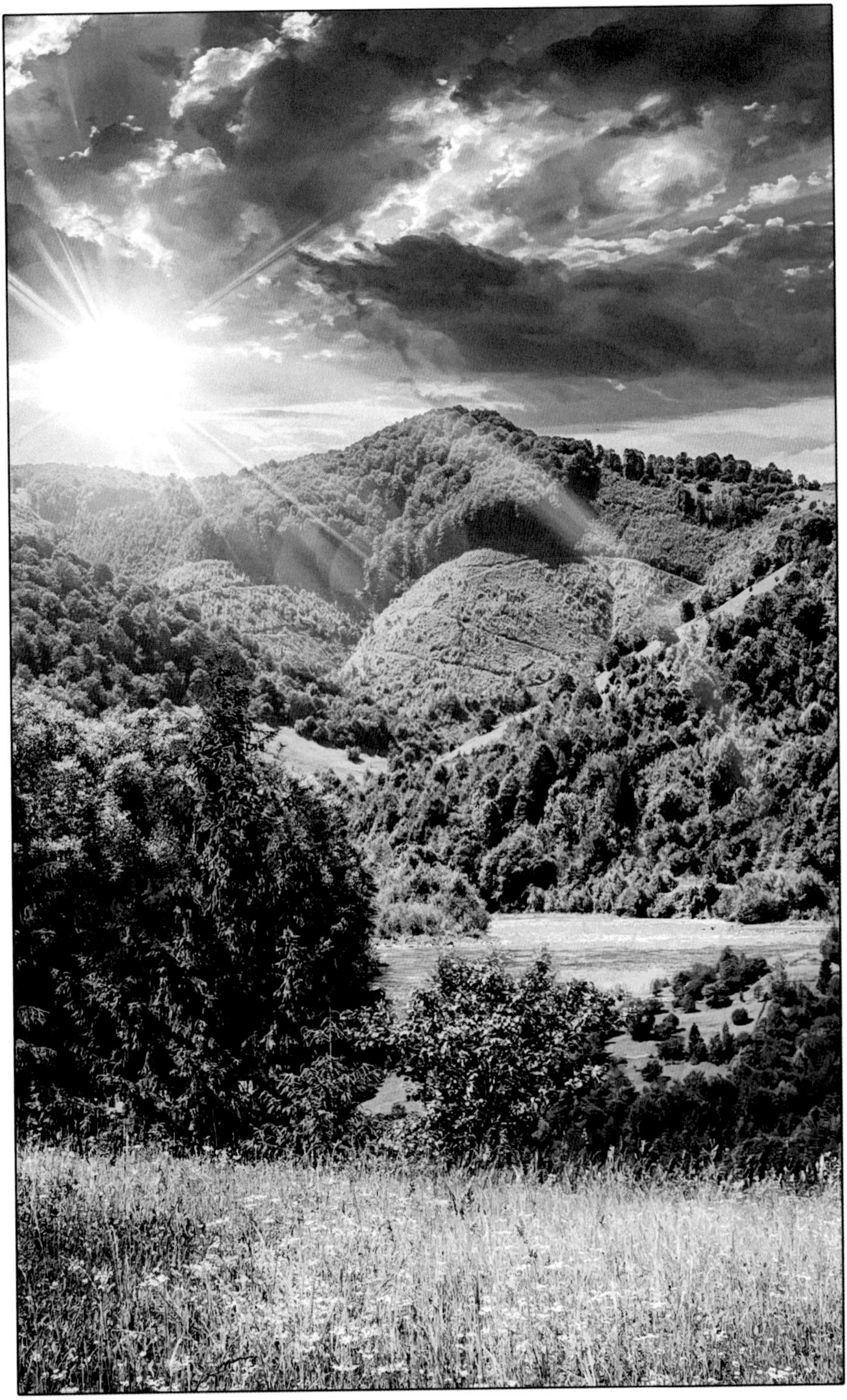

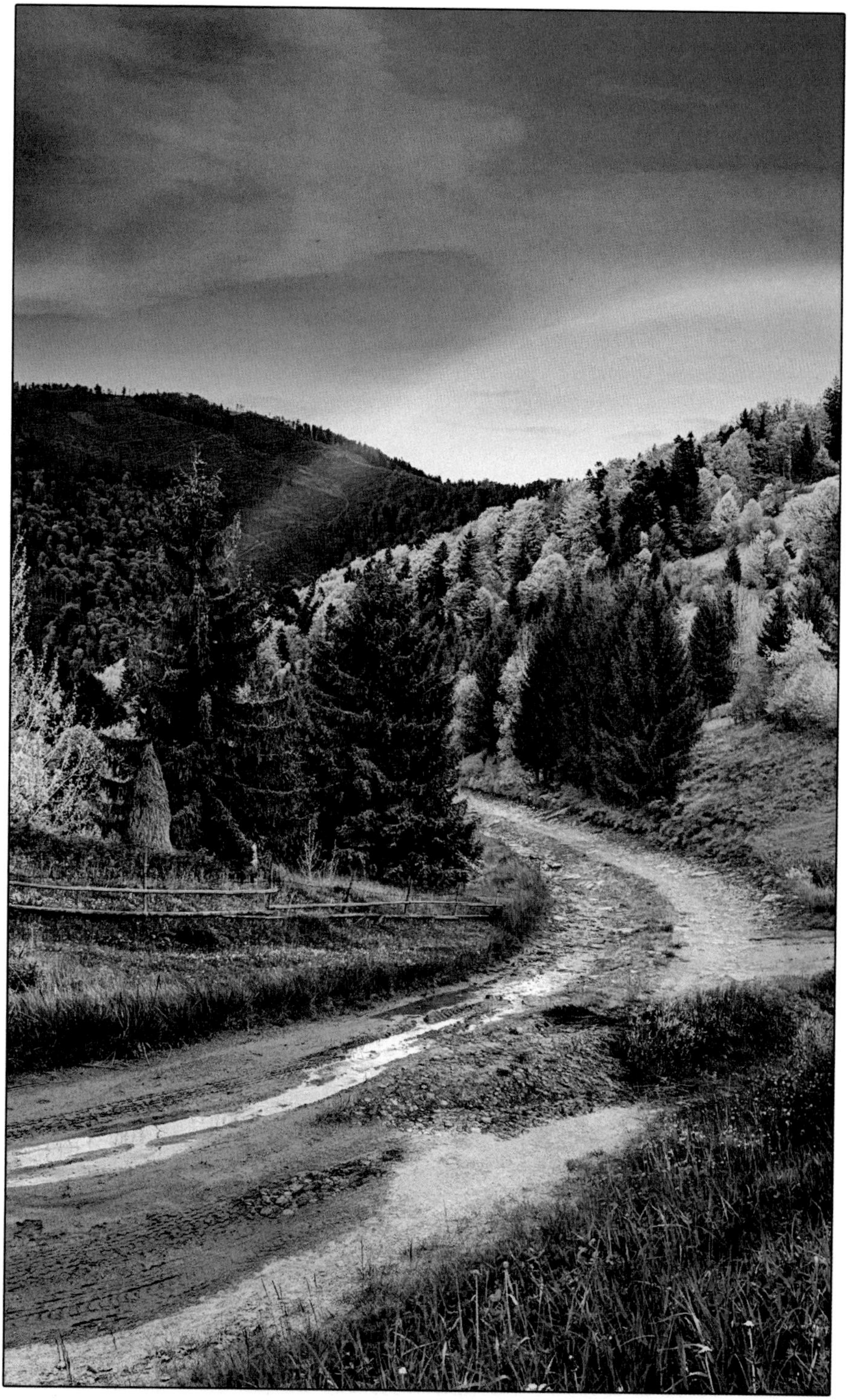

Made in the USA
Las Vegas, NV
27 December 2024

15439524R00026